D1995009

oekom verlag

Bibliografische Information der Deutschen Nationalbibliothek

Die Deutsche Nationalbibliothek verzeichnet diese Publikation in der Deutschen Nationalbibliografie; detaillierte bibliografische Daten sind im Internet über http://dnb.d-nb.de abrufbar.

---

oekom verlag, Gesellschaft für ökologische Kommunikation mbH
Waltherstraße 29, 80337 München

Umschlaggestaltung: Sandra Filic
Umschlagabbildung: photocase.de, eg
Druck: DIP – Digital-Druck Witten

Gedruckt auf FSC-zertifiziertem Papier

ISBN 978-3-86581-079-3

Regine Gerike

How to make sustainable transportation a reality

The development of three constitutive task fields for transportation

Preface

The aim of this work is to concretise the goal of sustainable transportation development while simultaneously considering its process character. Three task fields are developed and joined into a development corridor of sustainable transportation development. The resource task field forms the upper boundary, while the social task field forms the lower boundary. The allocative task field provides the rules for the scope between the boundaries. By concretising the task fields within a societal discussion, the concept of sustainable transportation development can be precisely described for concrete application.

This work contains firstly fundamental considerations about the concept of sustainable transportation development. These considerations will then be specified in order to show options for implementing the developed framework. Such implementation can only be realised by considering the particular circumstances which differ significantly from country to country and from region to region. Whenever it is necessary to refer to certain concrete local conditions, this will be done with the example of Germany in general, and/or Saxony in particular, since most of the empirical investigation underlying this work was done for Saxony.

The work is based on my doctoral thesis, which was submitted at the Dresden University of Technology and defended in April, 2005. The thesis has been updated, shortened and adapted for an international audience.

The author is grateful to everyone who has contributed to the work, especially to her colleagues from the Chair of Transportation Ecology and her family for their help and support with this work.

The thesis was financed by a grant from the Free State of Saxony to whom I also give sincere thanks. The work would not have been possible without this support.

Abstract

This work deals with the concept of sustainable transportation development. One important condition for the implementation of this concept is its operationalisation; i.e. the qualitative target of sustainability must be described by quantitative indicators. This is a difficult task because of the process character of the concept of sustainability. Concrete indicators are necessary in order to assess the status quo and changes in society: How one can find out if a measure is conducive to sustainability if this concept cannot be measured precisely?

The work presented here deals with the contradiction between the process character of sustainability and the demand for exact criteria by answering the following question: How can the concept of sustainable transportation development be specified while taking its process character into consideration?

In order to answer this question, the concept of needs is the central focus of this work: Sustainable development is regarded as development designed to meet the needs of people today and in the future. Needs are complex and constantly changing. Based on a theoretical discussion of this concept, the following task fields are established:

- Allocative task field: The market is a suitable instrument for identifying and satisfying needs. The aim of this task field is therefore to reduce market distortions in order to allow the qualities of the market mechanism to unfold unhindered.
- Social task field: Resulting from insufficient consideration of distributive aspects by the market mechanism, distributive task fields for sustainable transportation are required. Social aspects are covered by the social task field, the first distributive task field. The basis of sustainable transportation development is the providing of a basic transportation supply offered by governmental institutions. This supply has to guarantee the fulfilment of basic needs. It is described by minimum standards and completed by specific local planning. Therefore, the aim of this task field comprises the guarantee of a basic transportation supply.
- Resource task field: The object of the resource task field, the second distributive task field, is to rule the distribution of natural resources among generations and regions as the condition for the process of providing transportation services.

The three task fields developed are joined in a development corridor:

- The lower boundary is composed of a basic transportation supply to be guaranteed within the social task field. This basic transportation supply should not be fallen short.
- The upper limit of the corridor, which should not be exceeded, is composed of limits on carrying capacity to be formulated within the resource task field.
- The rules for all activities within the corridor should be defined by the allocative task field, the aim of which is to provide functioning market mechanisms.

In the next step, options for putting the development corridor into concrete terms are identified. If any of the suggested options are chosen within a societal discussion, the concept of sustainable transportation development can be described for concrete applications precisely.

Kurzfassung

Ausgangspunkt der Arbeit ist das Leitbild nachhaltiger Verkehrsentwicklung. Voraussetzung für die Umsetzung dieses qualitativen Leitbilds ist seine Operationalisierung, eine Aufgabe, die sich auf Grund des Prozesscharakters des Begriffs nachhaltiger Entwicklung als schwierig erweist. Eine Beschreibung dieses Begriffs durch konkrete, messbare Indikatoren ist aber notwendig, will man den Status quo sowie durchgeführte Maßnahmen anhand dieses Ziels bewerten. Die Arbeit versucht, den Widerspruch zwischen dem Prozesscharakter nachhaltiger Entwicklung und der Notwendigkeit, diese durch konkrete Indikatoren zu beschreiben, für den Verkehrsbereich einer Lösung näher zu bringen. Folgende zentrale Fragen ergeben sich für die Arbeit:

- Wie kann das Leitbild nachhaltiger Verkehrsentwicklung konkretisiert und dabei gleichzeitig dem Prozesscharakter des Nachhaltigkeitsbegriffs Rechnung getragen werden?
- Welche Empfehlungen lassen sich für Maßnahmen zur Förderung nachhaltiger Verkehrsentwicklung ableiten?

Dabei wird nachhaltige Entwicklung als eine an den Bedürfnissen der Menschen orientierte Entwicklung betrachtet. Die folgenden Aufgabenbereiche werden auf Basis einer bedürfnistheoretischen Diskussion erarbeitet:

- Allokationsbereich: Der Markt ist ein geeignetes Instrument zur Ermittlung und Befriedigung von Bedürfnissen. Das Ziel dieses Aufgabenbereichs besteht daher im Abbau von Marktunvollkommenheiten, um eine ungehinderte Entfaltung der Qualitäten des Marktmechanismus' zur Befriedigung menschlicher Bedürfnisse zu ermöglichen.
- Sozialer Aufgabenbereich: Aus der mangelnden Berücksichtigung von Verteilungsfragen durch den Marktmechanismus ergeben sich verteilungspolitische Aufgabenbereiche nachhaltiger Verkehrsentwicklung. Basis einer nachhaltigen Verkehrsentwicklung ist ein staatliches Angebot einer verkehrlichen Grundversorgung, durch welches die Befriedigung grundlegender Bedürfnisse gewährleistet wird. Das Ziel dieses Aufgabenbereichs besteht damit in der Gewährleistung einer verkehrlichen Grundversorgung. Dieses Angebot wird über Mindeststandards beschrieben und durch anwendungsspezifische Planungen ergänzt.

- Ressourcenbereich: Gegenstand des Ressourcenbereichs als zweiter verteilungspolitscher Aufgabenbereich ist die Regelung der Verteilung natürlicher Ressourcen als Anfangsausstattung für den Prozess zur Erstellung der Verkehrsleistungen.

Die erarbeiteten Aufgabenbereiche werden zu einem Entwicklungskorridor zusammengeführt:

- Die untere Begrenzung wird durch die im Rahmen des sozialen Aufgabenbereichs zu gewährleistende verkehrliche Grundversorgung gebildet. Diese sollte nicht unterschritten werden.
- Im Rahmen des Ressourcenbereichs zu formulierende Tragfähigkeitsgrenzen bilden die obere Begrenzung des Korridors und sollten nicht überschritten werden.
- Die Regeln für alle Aktivitäten innerhalb der Grenzen werden durch den Allokationsbereich vorgegeben, dessen Ziel die Gewährleistung funktionsfähiger Marktmechanismen ist.

Im Anschluss an die Erarbeitung des Entwicklungskorridors werden Optionen zu dessen Konkretisierung aufgezeigt. Werden Teile der erarbeiteten Optionen mit Hilfe einer gesellschaftlichen Diskussion ausgewählt, so ist damit für einzelne konkrete Anwendungsfälle eine abschließende Beschreibung des Ziels nachhaltiger Verkehrsentwicklung möglich.

Contents

A Introduction

A.1 Background

The concept of sustainable development was shaped and put into the political discussion in particular by the World Commission on Environment and Development, called the Brundtland-commission. At the Conference on Environment and Development in 1992 in Rio de Janeiro, 178 states agreed to this goal. Ever since, sustainability has become a new paradigm of political debates concerning environment and development (UBA, 2002).

In 2002, the federal government adopted a strategy of sustainable development for Germany called *"Perspectives for Germany."* In the introduction, the authors call sustainability a cross-sectional task and make it a basic principle of their policy (Bundesregierung 2002, p. 1). Consequently, the strategy of sustainable development has to be considered as the guideline for all fields of politics in Germany. This work deals with the transport sector, to which the strategy of sustainable development dedicated a special focus.

Since the Conference on the Environment and Development in Rio de Janeiro, there have been many attempts to operationalise[1] and to implement the concept of sustainability. Through these attempts it became obvious that it is not possible to directly implement sustainability. *"A sustainable economy and society can not be defined by minute criteria and managed like a detailed set of objectives. Rather than that, we have to emanate from future oriented learning, searching and designing, this process being necessarily characterised by a certain degree of openness and uncertainty."* (UBA, 2002, p. 1)

Such a process character of the concept of sustainability is contradictory to the aim of orienting measures in all fields of society to this concept. How to determine whether a measure is conducive to sustainability if this concept cannot be measured precisely? Detailed indicators are also necessary to determine and assess the status quo and societal changes with regard to sustainability.

---

1 The concept of operationalisation is a Latin word and stands for the specification of words, e.g. by using indicators which describe the word which is to be operationalised. In the present work the term operationalisation is used if qualitative terms should be made measurable.

Demands for exact criteria result in detailed catalogues of indicators that do not consider the process character of sustainability (Gudmundson, 2004; Jeon, 2005; Litman, 2005). This procedure is linked to several problems: As a result of such studies, there are many indicators. However, the handling of target conflicts as well as the weighting of the indicators among each other often remains unclear (Surburg, 2002). Sometimes, indicators are developed only for parts of the sustainable development concept and the interaction with other fields of this concept remains open (UBA, 2001). The consequence is a wide scope of interpretation of the studies' results used by different interest groups to interpret their confessed aims into the indicators.

The aim of this work is to show possibilities for the transport sector to resolve the contradiction between the process character of sustainability, on the one hand, and the demand for a precisely measurable aim on the other.

This results in the following central questions for the present study:

- How can the concept of sustainable transportation development be concretised while simultaneously taking the process character of this concept into consideration?
- Which recommendations for the implementation of measures to encourage sustainable development can be derived?

A.2 Approach

The first step is to delineate the concept of sustainability for the present study. This is a condition for concretising sustainable transportation – that is, for answering the first question. The result of this first step is that sustainable development corresponds to development that meets the needs of present and future generations. Consequently, the concept of needs will form the centre of the following argumentation: The starting point of the present study is the aim of a transport development, which is oriented to the needs of the people living today and in the future.

In order to concretise this aim, one has to develop quantitative sub-goals and indicators. Options for this are developed in the present work by using “task fields”; the concept of sustainable transportation is subdivided into three task fields. By concretising these task fields, this qualitative goal can be made manageable for planning activities. By joining the task fields, a development corridor is established, which provides freely designable scope for the societal searching and discussion process mentioned above.

Figure 1 illustrates the chosen approach. Two task fields form the boarders of the corridor. They must be met to ensure the advancement of sustainable development. The third task field provides the rules for the development within the boarders. By choosing this approach, the process character of the concept of sustainability is taken into account and space for the above mentioned “*future oriented learning, searching and designing*” is left.

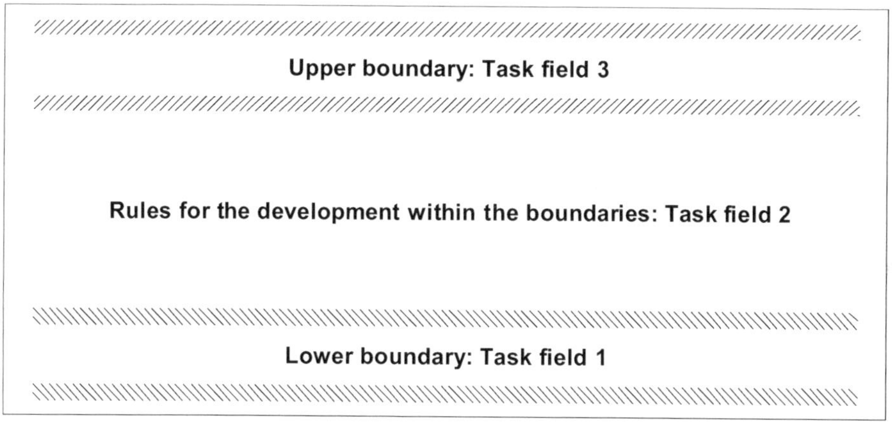

Figure 1: Development corridor of sustainable development – the aim of this work.

Thus, this work contains in its first parts (A and B) fundamental considerations about the concept of sustainable transportation development. In the third part of the work (part C) the insights gained so far will be specified with the aim of showing options for implementing the developed framework. Such implementation can only be realised by considering the particular circumstances which differ significantly from country to country and region to region. Whenever it is necessary to refer to certain concrete local conditions, this will be done with the example of Germany in general, and/or Saxony in particular, since most of the empirical investigation underlying this work was done for Saxony.

Which of the planning process phases does the work deal with? It deals with the phase of problem analysis and definition, and in this phase, especially with the development of guidelines and targets (FGSV, 2000; Litman, 2006c). Mastering this phase is an important prerequisite for all further steps: the status quo can only be assessed if there are quantitative criteria and indicators available. Such indicators form the basis for the following phases of the planning process: investigation of measures, assessment and decision, implementation and supervision of the impacts of the implemented measures.

By asking these questions, the work is placed on the border of science and politics: The task of (transport) policy is the setting of exact goals as well as the choice of measures for reaching them. Science can give recommendations for conceptualising packages of suitable measures to reach the set goals. The German Society for Research in Transport Sciences writes concerning this point: "*The task of each transportation planning is the target oriented, systematic, foresighted and informed preparation of decisions and actions which should influence the transport system according to the respective aims.*" (FGSV, 2000, p. 3) The present work fits into this framework.

A.3 Outline

The previously presented approach results in the following structure:

Part A, "Introduction," introduces the problems to be dealt with: The topic of the work is presented and specified. The structure of the work is detailed.

Part B carries the title "**Corridor of sustainable transportation development**." Firstly, in chapter B.1, the concept of sustainability is discussed. Then, in chapter B.2, the following relevant transport terms are defined: "mobility," "transport," "accessibility" and "access." Based on a theoretical discussion of the concept of needs in chapter B.3, the task fields are established in chapter B.4.2 and joined into a development corridor in chapter B.4.3.

In **part C, "Options for concretising the development corridor,"** possibilities for making the task fields concrete parts of the developed corridor are analysed. The structure of this part is similar to the three tasks fields established in part B: Options for putting each task field into concrete terms are shown. In chapter C.4, recommendations on how to implement sustainable transportation development are derived. In chapter C.5, consequences of the knowledge obtained for the assessment of measures are discussed.

Part D, "Conclusions," summarises the most important results of the work. Open questions are discussed. Figure 2 shows the course of the work.

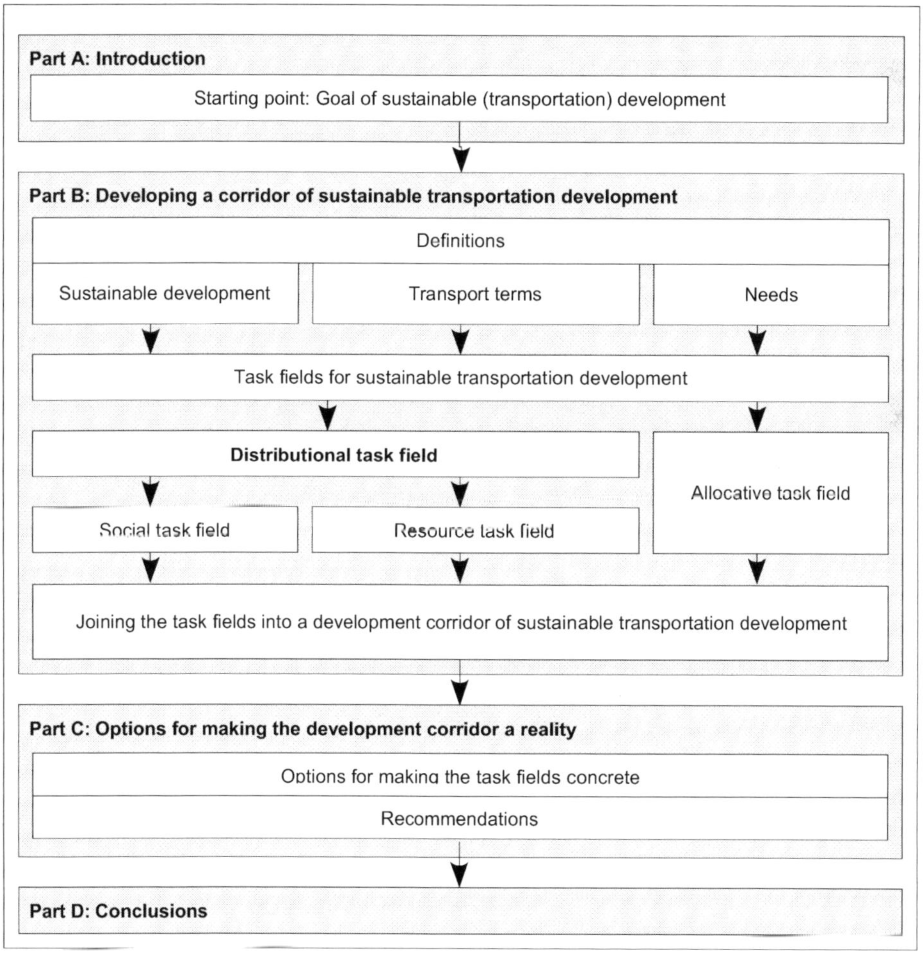

Figure 2: Course of work.

A.4 Reader's guide

Figure 3 serves to guide the reader throughout the work and sums up the structure of the work. Part A serves as an introduction and part D as conclusions. These two parts form the frame for the actual development of the content in parts B and C and therefore are not shown in the graphic. Figure 3 will be shown in the beginning of each part of the work to illustrate the status of work and the tasks to be done in the following part. This figure, as well as the text parts marked by , make navigation through the work easier and serve as guidance for the reader. Conclusions and text passages which are particularly important for the development of work are marked by the sign .

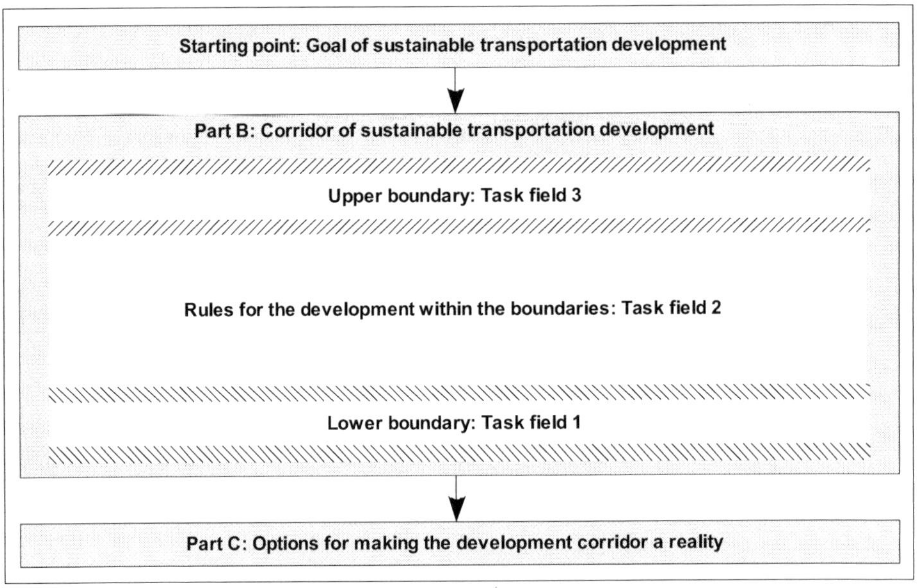

Figure 3: Overview of the steps of the study.

B Corridor of sustainable transportation development

In part B the relevant terms are first defined to ensure a clear conceptual basis for the following chapters. The concept of sustainability is delineated in chapter B.1. In chapter B.2 relevant transport terms are defined. Establishing a stable conceptual basis is vital in order to be able to address the question of which variables sustainable transportation development should focus on. Should we focus on "mobility" in order to establish a sustainable transportation system? Are transport indicators or the term "accessibility" more suitable? Answering these questions is an important prerequisite for all further work.

In the following chapters, the task fields are established: The concept of needs is discussed in chapter B.3 in order to form the basis for deriving the task fields in chapter B.4.2. In chapter B.4.3 the task fields are joined into a development corridor. As a result of part B, the basic structure of the development corridor will have been developed. Figure 4 clarifies the tasks of part B.

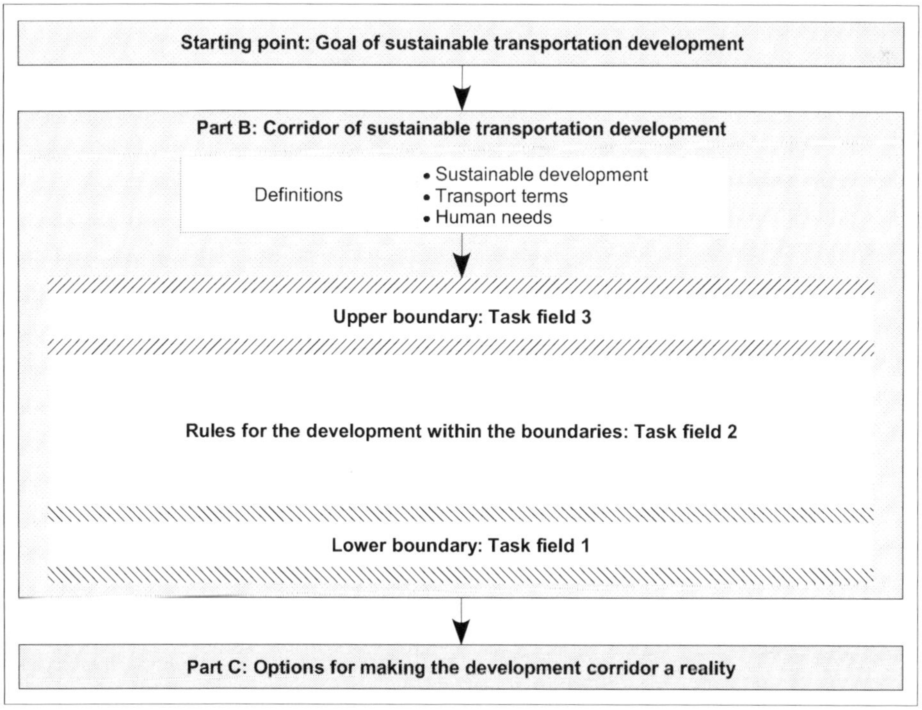

Figure 4: Overview of the steps of the study – Part B.

B.1 The concept of sustainable development – Current discussion and definition

The concept of sustainable development came originally from forestry. Hanns Carl von Carlowitz (1713) described forest management aiming at long-term success in his book "*Sylvicultura Oeconomica. Die Naturgemäße Anweisung zur wilden Baumzucht*": No more wood should be extracted from the forest then would grow again in it.[2]

The starting point for the present discussion on sustainability is above all the work done by the World Commission on Environment and Development (WCED) established by the United Nations (UN).[3] In 1987, this commission published the report "*Our common future*" (Brundtland-Commission, 1987) which is often called the "Brundtland-Report," referring to the chairwoman of the WCED, former Prime Minister of Norway Gro Harlem Brundtland. The report uses the following definition of the term "sustainable development":

> "*Sustainable development is development that meets the needs of the present without compromising the ability of future generations to meet their own needs.*" (Brundtland-Commission, 1987, p. 24)[4]

This definition leaves room for different interpretations. Sometimes, its diffuseness is criticised. Ewers writes: "Sustainable development does not present itself as a final concept but rather as a behavioural instruction to the political actors to find out the respective boundaries of the system." (Ewers, 1996, p. 205)

However, the anthropocentric character of the Brundtland definition is obvious: People and their needs are put at the centre of the definition. The basic orientation to a principle of intra- and intergenerational justice is another important characteristic of the definition which lays claim to meeting the needs of people even in future generations.

In welfare economics, various tools were developed to establish criteria for configuring politics aimed at meeting human needs (Barr, 1998; Dolgoff, 2006; Feldmann,

---

2 See also Radke, 1999 for the history of the idea of sustainable development.

3 Schley (2001) and Wheeler (2004) give an overview of the discussion on sustainability. UBA (1997, 2002) describe the debate on sustainability in Germany. See http://www.nachhaltigkeitsrat.de for actions of the German council on sustainable development established by the German government.

4 See Diefenbacher, 2001 for an overview of different definitions and delimitations of the concept of sustainability.

1997; Moore, 2006; Pigou, 2006). This goal is operationalised by the term "utility" which is defined as "*the characteristic of a good to meet the needs of people.*" (Blum 2000, p. 9)

Consequently, the concept of utility is a yardstick for comparing different packages of consumption. The different goods and services are transformed into a uniform denominator. According to welfare theory, the aim of a household is to maximise its utility under the constraint of a given income usable for consumption. The utility is derived from the subjective value in use and stands for the "usefulness" of things for certain individuals depending on time and location. Utility functions describe the utility of certain individuals dependent on quality and quantity of goods used.[5] Social Welfare Functions (SWF) may be formed by aggregating individual utility functions. SWF make it possible to rank different allocations in an economy.[6]

According to the Brundtland definition, which is oriented to the concept of needs, sustainable development may be operationalised under these assumptions as a growth path over present and future generations[7] which maximises an intergenerational social welfare function (Pearce, 1990; Wellisch, 2000; Wieland, 2002). Consequently, according to welfare theory, the aim of economic policies is to meet the needs of people as well as possible. Value judgements, constraints derived from equity reflections and environmental and geophysical constraints are important considerations for the calculations (Nutzinger, 1996; Pearce, 1990).

By setting those scientific constraints, concepts of weak sustainability to concepts of strong sustainability may be modelled by welfare economic instruments.[8] These concepts are usually anthropocentric ones as well. Some authors support the opinion that concepts of strong sustainability are related to a transition from an anthropocentric to a biocentric point of view.[9]

---

5 For the distinction between ordinal and cardinal measurements of utility see Blum, 2000; Kreuzburg, 1999; Statistisches Bundesamt 1996; Varian, 2004.

6 The term allocation stands for the assignment of factors of production and/or goods in the economic process; see Blum, 2000.

7 The time horizon may be finite as well as infinite.

8 These concepts are discussed especially in natural sciences. For the subdivision of concepts of sustainability see Diefenbacher, 2001; Lerch, 2000; Wheeler, 2004. See Lerch, 2000; Voß, 2002 for criticism concerning the concept of strong sustainability. See Daly, 1992; UBA, 1997 for rules of management.

9 This would mean putting the needs of people second to the concerns of nature. Both positions in their pure form lead to unrealistic consequences, so that in the literature mainly mixed positions are found. This leads to the thesis of the convergence of the two positions, which is supported by various authors; see Lerch, 2000; WBGU, 1999.

The concepts can be distinguished by their claim on the beneficial potential to be passed to future generations. Some models claim the transmission of a non-declining national income (extremely weak sustainability); others claim the transmission of an overall constant stock of natural and artificial capital with unrestricted combinations of the two components (weak sustainability); a third group claims the transmission of a least possible stock of (critical) natural capital (critical sustainability); and a final group the transmission of a constant natural capital (strong sustainability).

There is wide agreement in literature that the concept of sustainable development is based on three pillars:

- The social pillar reflects the demand for intra- and intergenerational justice: People of different generations as well as people of different regions should have equal chances.
- The ecological pillar challenges the preservation of the environment.
- The economic pillar points to the material wealth of people.

Some authors include a fourth pillar, the institutional pillar, which claims the necessity of institutional changes (Diefenbacher, 2001).

The question of whether the pillars have equal importance or should be regarded in a hierarchical way by assigning different priorities to them, lacks a consensus in literature. Developing countries, in particular, give priority to social and economic aspects by claiming that highly-developed industrial nations have to make special effort to facilitate sustainable development and therefore should carry the main financial burdens. The debate on sustainability in natural sciences prioritises the solution of ecological problems using the argument that sustainable development may only be implemented if nature as the basis for all life is not endangered. Daly (1996) developed the following hierarchy of aims:

- The main priority is assigned to the problem of scale: The use of natural resources has to be adjusted to the ecological carrying capacity.
- Next, questions about a fair distribution of the natural resources within the ecological carrying capacity are posed. This point is divided into an intertemporal and an international component.

- Finally, there are allocation problems to be solved. This is possible through the market mechanism providing it works with "true" prices, i.e. with prices that include internal and external costs.

This hierarchy shows an approach for efficiently using the scope given by the "ecological carrying capacity." Therefore, it is a more practical approach than equal weighing of the three pillars of sustainable development, because in the latter case target conflicts between the different pillars remain. Furthermore, a hierarchical analysis seems to be the only way of considering the growing environmental problems. Human interventions have reached a dimension in which the natural basis for life appears increasingly endangered. This fact may also be considered by giving great weight to ecological aspects within a non-hierarchical analysis of the three aspects. This would lead implicitly to an assimilation of hierarchical versus non-hierarchical approaches.

The Federal Environment Agency writes: *"All economic activity and therefore the wealth in the classical sense stands under the restriction of the ecological carrying capacity, because development and wealth are only possible within the space left by nature as the basis for life. Therefore, the carrying capacity of the natural household has to be accepted as the last barrier for all kinds of human activity that must not be passed over. The only question is how to best use the remaining space."* (UBA, 2002, p. 2)

For the present work, the Brundtland definition is used as the basis for the concept of sustainability, since it is widespread and highly recognised. This definition is marked by an anthropocentric character and therefore by an orientation to human needs. Consequently, the orientation to the needs of people is put at the centre of the following chapters; sustainable development is regarded as development oriented to the needs of people, i.e. to the needs of present and of future generations.

The basis of the following chapters is an anthropocentric concept of sustainability which puts the needs of present and future people at the centre of analysis.

The task of the following chapters is to develop methods to concretise the delineated concept of sustainability in order to answer the questions posed at the beginning of work. These questions can now be reformulated as follows: Is the concept of needs an appropriate target figure for measures within the transport sector? How can a transport development which aims at meeting human needs be concretised? Which requirements should be fulfilled by measures oriented to the defined objective?

B.2 Definition of transport terms

The philosopher Ludwig Wittgenstein (1994) remarked that the meaning of terms shows up in their use. An associated use of the terms "mobility," "transport," "accessibility" and "access" means that they are linked. They describe different aspects of the movements of people and goods in space and time. Can the terms therefore be used synonymously? If that is not possible, where are the differences then, and how can the terms be differentiated from each other?

Researching the relevant literature, two things become clear (Axhausen, 2007; Gerike, 2005; Litman, 2005b):

- The ideas indicated by the terms overlap.
- There are substantially different views concerning the precise ideas behind the terms.

This becomes particularly apparent in the case of the terms mobility and transport, both of which describe the movements of goods and people. In what follows, the spectrum of the content is defined, which all transport terms should cover. The following four levels should be included in a systematic of transport terms:

- OPTIONS: all possibilities people have to move and to realise activities,
- TRANSPORT: all impacts of going to destinations for realising activities: trips, time, money, resources etc.
- ACTIVITIES: number and type of activities realised through the transport,
- NEEDS: the needs which are satisfied through this realisation of activities.

By considering the last two points of activities realised alongside certain movements and needs satisfied by the activities, the "classical" spectrum of transport terms with a focus on the movement itself is expanded. This expansion is owing to the goal of sustainable transportation development that was defined as development aiming at satisfying the needs of people. A sound conceptual basis, including the needs satisfied by certain transport activities, is necessary in order to concretise the goal of sustainable transportation development.

Furthermore, there is great potential for designing environmentally friendly transport in considering realised activities and needs satisfied. The same activity can be realised with more or less, and in some cases, even without transport. This interface between movement and activities becomes vital by looking at transport in its serving function as a means for enabling people to satisfy their needs. The goal, therefore, should be to design a transport system that helps people satisfy their needs as well as possible with as little transport cost and effort as possible. One would leave out the actual benefits of transport by omitting realised activities and needs satisfied.

There is another interface between activities realised and needs satisfied: With the same activity, different needs can be satisfied. Going for lunch might only satisfy hunger but in other cases it might satisfy needs for communication, affection and self-esteem. Working might only be a means for gaining money, but it might also satisfy the same additional needs as above.

Consequently, two interfaces are vital for designing sustainable transportation development: the interface between activities and transport, on the one hand, and between needs satisfied and activities realised, on the other.

Table 1 gives an overview of the current discussion in literature concerning the four points listed above:

Subject of transport terms:	**To be described in literature mainly by the following terms:**	**Possible indicators:**
Options	Access, accessibility	Accessibility measures like the number of destinations to be reached with certain cost and effort
Transport (expendi-ture)	Mobility, transport, transportation, traffic	Number and length of the realised trips, time spent, vehicle kilometres travelled, environmental damages caused
Number and type of realised activities	Access	Number and type of realised activities
Needs	Mobility or transport needs	Satisfy hunger, safety, affection, self-esteem as primary need; need to move to destinations where needs can be satisfied as secondary need

Table 1: Content of transport terms in literature.

For the following lines of argumentation, the terms mobility, transport, transportation and traffic are used to describe movements including all inputs and impacts. The borders between the terms are blurry, with the following definitions used as the basis in this work:

Mobility covers individual-related indicators: number of trips, time spent and distances covered. It can likewise be applied to freight transport by indicating ton kilometres, number of trips and distances covered. This definition is common in German-speaking areas.

Traffic stands for vehicle-related items like vehicle miles travelled and includes all environmental impacts of movement.

The terms transport and transportation stand for the whole system facilitating the movement of people and goods and are described mainly be aggregated indicators: length and type of infrastructure, number and type of vehicles, etc. The term transport can also be used to describe movement on an aggregated level.

Accessibility stands not for movement but for options for movement and is described by the number, kind and location of opportunities people have as spatial components and by options for reaching the opportunities as transport components. Accessibility can be determined by the planner without asking the affected people; it always refers to a certain place and certain groups of people.

The term access should be strictly separated from accessibility and describes the activities realised. The distinction between access and the terms describing movement itself is found in the different ways one individual realises the same activity programme. The following general relationship exists: For completing an activity programme of x outside activities, which is to begin and end at the dwelling place, a minimum of x + 1 trips and a maximum of 2 x trips are necessary. The concrete number of realised trips depends on the temporal-spatial coordination of the transport user: If one drives to work in the morning, for instance, and directly home in the evening, then for the activity "work," two trips were realised. If one goes shopping on the way back, goes to the hairdresser and picks up a child from day care, then four activities are connected with five trips: dwelling → work → shopping → hairdresser → day care → dwelling. In this case, for one activity an average of 1.25 trips were necessary.

This example illustrates that one activity can be realised at different transport cost and effort. Differences exist both in the number of trips realised and in the costs related to the trips.

Human needs are the last level to cover and, as the central focus of sustainable transportation development, do not need an extra term. They are simply referred to as human needs in this work. We have to distinguish between primary needs, like psychological or safety needs, and between mobility needs as the so-called secondary or derived needs; people must be able to reach the destinations where they can satisfy their primary needs. Planning for sustainable transportation development must not be restricted to mobility needs. It is not enough to be able to move and to reach various locations; there have to be opportunities for satisfying human needs at these locations: shops, schools etc. Here the link between transport and spatial planning is addressed: destinations need to exist; their quality needs to be high enough that people are able to satisfy their needs there; and there must be a transport system which enables people to reach the existing destinations.

Figure 5 illustrates how the terms are connected according to the discussed definitions.

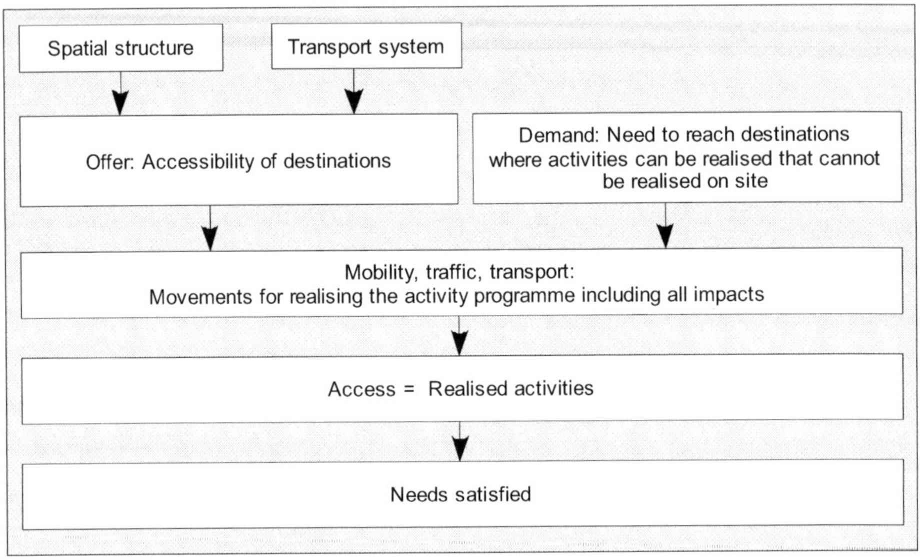

Figure 5: Systematic of the transport terms used in this work.

B.3 The concept of "human needs"

> Because of the orientation of the concept of sustainable development to the needs of people as it is used in the present work, the concept of needs must be discussed and delineated. This will be done in chapter B.3.

"Needs are feelings of scarcity related to the striving for getting rid of them." (Herrmann, 1870, p. 30) Needs are the reason for any action, and therefore they are the topic of everyday reflections and everyone's planning. Different sciences have dealt intensively with the concept of needs since the Enlightenment. Psychologists investigate which needs people perceive, how needs change over the course of life and how they are influenced by which reasons (Hondrich, 1983; Schlag, 2002a, 2002b, 2003). Economists analyse the question of how needs become real demands and how to predict and to influence these demands (Gottl-Ottlilienfeld, 1928; Wellisch, 2000). Philosophers deal with fundamental questions like the delineation of the concepts of needs, motive and drive as well as the question of whether and under

which conditions people realise their "true" needs (Berger, 1992; Scherhorn, 1959; Spinner, 1976; Wiggins, 1991).

In the literature of transport sciences, the concept of needs is found rather seldom. There are older approaches to planning for the needs of people that concentrate mainly on social disadvantages caused by the transport system (Albrecht, 1977; Heinemann-Knoch, 1977). In Great Britain, planning for the needs of people is discussed in the context of questions of social exclusion (Social Exclusion Unit, 2003). Furthermore, research on the origins of transportation demand relies on the concept of needs. This research aims at predicting transport behaviour of different groups of people (Axhausen, 2007; Ettema, 1997).

In the following chapters, a short interdisciplinary introduction to the discussion of needs will be given, always looking at the relevant questions for the present investigation: How can the aim of sustainable transportation development be concretised by regarding it as development aimed at meeting the needs of people?

Firstly, in chapter B.3.1, different approaches found in literature are presented to systemise the needs of people. Next, in chapters B.3.2 to B.3.4, different questions related to the concept of needs and relevant to the present work are discussed. This is done without comments in these chapters. In chapter B.4.1, the theoretical reflections are summarised and conclusions are drawn referring to all parts of chapter B.3.

The theoretical discussion of the concept of needs forms the basis for developing the task fields for sustainable transportation development in chapter B.4.2, as well as for concretising them in part C of the work.

B.3.1 Approaches to systemise human needs

Human needs are complex. People have many different needs. There are conflicts within the needs of one individual: between the need for more spare time and the wish to obtain more money, for instance. Needs are changeable and marked by society. The expectation for satisfying the need for shelter differs, for instance, from the highlands in South America to Central Europe. The consequence of this complexity is that there is no generally accepted theory of needs. There are manifold approaches for systemising and explaining needs and their changes (Erikson, 1968;

Galtung, 1980; Gasieth, 1981; Knoll, 1977; Mallmann, 1980; Schlag, 2002, 2002b; Wirz, 1993). Next, an overview of this discussion will be given with a focus on the following approaches:

- Those which represent systematic comprehensive approaches
- Those which are particularly influential
- Those which claim to scientifically justify planning corresponding human needs

These concepts are divided according to Mussel (1992) into approaches which regard needs above all a) as behavioural incentive, b) as objective human and societal necessity or c) as aspects of human self-development. The boarders between the concepts cannot be clearly drawn. Rather, the different concepts represent a continuum, whose poles will be described in the following chapters.

B.3.1.1 Needs as behavioural drive: Psychological approaches

Representatives of this direction of primarily psychological research regard needs as *"drives of scarcity"* that are responsible for human behaviour and are *"in the service of stopping unwanted (physiological or psychological) states in human organisms. The aim of satisfying needs is to re-establish a state of peacefulness, suitability and balance."* (Krech, 1968, p. 202) Consequently, this definition assumes that individuals are aware of their lacks and that they can describe these lacks precisely. Therefore, human behaviour is directed by a multitude of inner driving forces, which are also called motivating energy.

Probably, the most widespread approach is the "pyramid of needs," developed by Maslow (1987).[10] Maslow divided needs into a hierarchical structure: needs of lower levels must be satisfied before needs of the respective higher level become relevant.[11] All needs of the different levels may be satisfied completely with the exception of the highest level: the need for self-realisation. This need forms the top of the pyramid and is open to the top. It can never be satisfied completely; there is no

---

[10] The scheme of Erik Allardt is a further approach to systemising human needs that is widely used for the empirical measurement of wealth in Germany, see Hauser, 1996.

[11] The idea of using a hierarchical structure to systemise human needs was not created by Maslow, but his system is the first comprehensive and well-known approach. Even Marx worked with a hierarchical structure of needs, see Marx, 1976a, b, 1985.

“end” to these needs at the top of the pyramid of needs. Figure 6 shows the different levels of the pyramid.

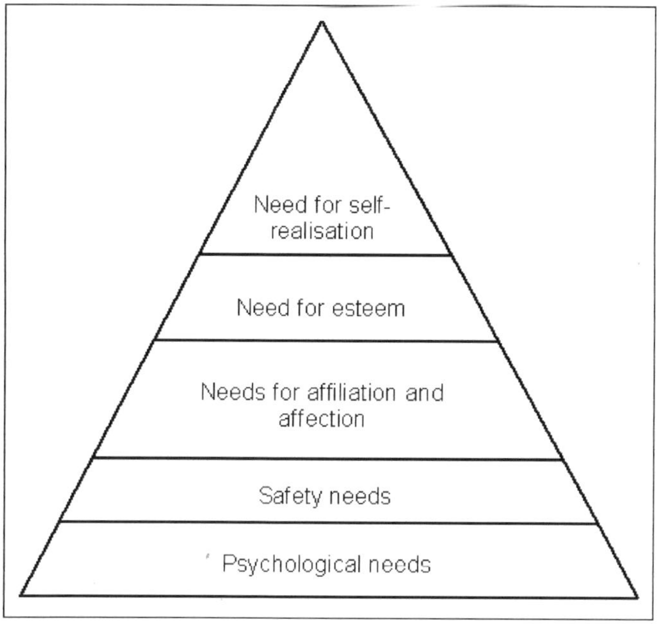

Figure 6: Hierarchy of needs (Becker, 1999; Maslow, 1981; Schlag, 2002a).

The lowest level of needs, the physiological needs, includes all needs related to physical survival like nourishment, clothing, shelter etc. Maslow described these needs as *“the most powerful of all”: “If these needs are not fulfilled and the organism is ruled by the physiological needs, all other needs can simply stop existing or they are pushed to the background.” “The wish to write poems, the desire for a new car, the interest in history, the wish for a new pair of shoes are forgotten in the extreme case or become secondary. For those who are extremely hungry, no interest exists other than nourishment. They dream of nourishment, think of nourishment, their feelings deal with nourishment, they perceive only nourishment and claim for nourishment.”* (Maslow, 1987, p. 63 f.)

The next level, the safety needs, includes order, protection, predictability of danger, reliability of environment and freedom from fear. Needs for affection, for relatedness to a group or territory, interpersonal relations and sociability belong to the third level. The fourth level of the hierarchy refers to self-esteem as well as to the esteem of others. The topmost level, the need for self-realisation, describes the entitlement to development that meets personal preferences and abilities. It manifests itself very differently depending on the affected individual and the exterior circumstances.

According to Maslow, all people pass through all of these needs during their development. Therefore the growth of personality can be described as a sequence of waves clarifying the increasing and decreasing importance of certain levels of needs. Physiological needs stand in the foreground during the first years of life. Step by step, the physiological needs are pushed to the background by higher levels of needs. When they are elderly, humans strive increasingly for self-realisation.

The hierarchy of needs is widespread because of its clarity and understandability. Criticism discussed in literature points to the hierarchical division,[12] the assumption of trends to higher needs which is rooted in developmental psychology (Meyer-Abich, 1979; Prechtl, 1983; Schlag, 2002b) and the vague phrasing of the levels of needs. Security needs, for instance, can have completely different characteristics: Humans have the need for security against violence, for a steady income, for a stable job. All these completely different fields rank among the need category "security." In addition, the hierarchy system is not regarded as complete. It mentions no need for power and achievement, for example.

B.3.1.2 Needs as objective human and societal necessity

Carl Menger, the founder of the school of marginal utility, defines needs as *"the necessity of preservation and harmonic development of human nature in its totality."* (Menger, 1923, p. 3) Needs are regarded as objective necessity which is valid independently of specific individuals. Beyond this, there is the assumption that it is possible to identify the needs of people through outside circumstances. Needs exist independently of people's awareness and therefore can only sometimes be directly identified.[13] Many people suffering from diabetes do not feel or do not know about their disease, for instance. If the disease exceeds a certain threshold, the affected individuals become aware of the consequences, but without the diagnosis of a specialist they still know neither the reasons for their condition nor the options for therapy, i.e. for satisfying a need, which only appears through symptoms.

Consequently, needs may be better identified not by asking the affected individuals but rather by looking at their behaviour. Another option to identify human needs is

[12] Maslow (1987), himself, points out that the hierarchy should be interpreted as levels with decreasing urgency: The urgency of physiological needs decreases the more they are fulfilled, but nevertheless the need for nourishment is present, even if higher needs are more important, because the satisfaction of the need for nourishment is ensured.

[13] See Hondrich, 1983 for the discussion of conscious and unconscious needs.

to derive them from theoretical reflections based on certain moral concepts. The delineation between the first and the second approach regarding the concept of needs may be summed up as follows: Approaches regarding needs as behavioural drive try to answer the question of what we want, whereas the representatives of the second approach describe what we need through the concept of needs (Birnbacher, 1979). The most important distinction is that the condition of "needing" something is always a purpose. To "want" something like health, satisfaction and well-being is not necessarily related to a certain purpose.

Hence, the concept of needs in the sense of "wanting" is used purely descriptively to describe what people wish for: latently or manifestly, consciously or unconsciously. Describing the concept of needs by "needing" something has a normative character: a purpose is assumed to which the needs are connected. The aim is to reach the purpose beneath, which has to be set by the affected individuals, themselves, or by somebody else like a teacher, politician or philosopher. Accordingly, the first approach starts with the people and their needs, while the second approach starts with an aim which must be formulated by society. What people need in order to reach the aim must be determined.[14]

The logical consequence of regarding needs as objective necessities is that the determination of needs may be and should be left to experts. For the inclusion of people, it is sufficient to conduct surveys in order to determine indicators of wealth and satisfaction. The objective and subjective indicators determined in this way are appropriate target figures of planning; ongoing forms of participation are not necessary (Mallmann, 1980). The exchange between people and their environment becomes restricted to the satisfaction of their needs determined externally without involving them in the discovery of their needs. Only the knowledge of the "functional principles" of people is necessary in order to manage the society purposefully.

Planned economies, in which the production as well as the setting of prices are controlled centrally, are based on this approach. Meeting the needs of people is denoted by many authors as the aim of this central control (Haustein, 1976).

[14] Mallmann uses the aim of quality of life, which he considers equal to a very comprehensive understanding of health, see Mussel, 1992 for this discussion.

B.3.1.3 Needs as aspects of human self-development

The idea of a mutual exchange between individuals and society is the most important characteristic of this way of thinking about the concept of needs: *"Individuals produce their own world and thus become the subject of their own creation. The individual is subject as well as object of history, neither only the one nor only the other."* (Israel, 1985, p. 39) This interplay is described by the concept of self-development[15] of human beings.[16]

Marx was the first to use the concept of self-development related to the concept of human needs. Like the representatives of psychological approaches discussed in chapter B.3.1.1, Marx stated that needs are the driving force behind human behaviour. By denying the separation between individual and society, he changed the view from needs as a starting point and aim of action to the process of acting. Consequently, he focused on the exchange between people, society and nature. According to Marx, it is a human need to become a subject in this exchange. Further needs develop by satisfying needs and creating instruments and institutions for this (Marx, 1976a, b, 1983, 1985). Humans become a product of their own creation, a societal product. On the other hand, society is a product of human being, as well.

Mead is a further supporter of this way of thinking. Like Marx, he does not regard the individual and society as separate units but as aspects of the respective other. The development of individual identity depends on how the individual is involved in societal processes: *"Getting in the activity of the whole society into the experience of any involved individual is the crucial basis and condition for the complete development of the identity of individuals."* (Mead, 1991, p. 53)

This "*getting in*" of societal activity is one side of the exchange. The influence of the individual on societal processes is the other side: *"We must not forget the ability to respond to society and insist on changing gestures of society."* (Mead, 1991, p. 136) Consequently, human behaviour is never determined completely by society.

---

[15] See Mussel, 1992 for further explanation concerning the concept of self-generation.

[16] Jörissen et al. (1999: 89 ff.) argue in the same way to describe the social dimension of sustainability. For that, they refer to the "theory of structuring" and the "duality of structure" developed by Giddens.

Everybody contributes to the genesis, preservation and changing of society by bringing in their experience, ideas and thoughts: *"We permanently change our societal system in some aspects and we can do this in an intelligent way because we are able to think."* (Mead, 1991, p. 137)

B.3.2 Individual versus societal needs

In the following chapter, the concept of societal needs will be discussed. Here, the question is addressed of whether needs exist that go beyond the needs of the individuals the society comprises.

In literature, opinions differ on the question of whether societal needs exist at all (Hondrich, 1983). Some authors argue that even collective decisions can be attributed to individual behaviour. Therefore, needs can only be related to individuals from the beginning. Other authors describe societal needs like the need for a stable legal system which seems to contradict the individual need for maximal freedom. Another example is the societal need for an intact and livable environment, which seems to stand in contradiction to the wish of individuals for maximal use of that environment.

All examples describe situations in which conflicts occur. Conflicts within the need systems of each individual overlap with conflicts between the needs of different individuals. An example of an interpersonal conflict concerning the use of the environment is a farmer's need for clean air which contradicts the drivers' need on the motorway bordering the farmland. The drivers' need air to burn fuel in their engines as much as the farmer's plants need clean air to grow.

These interpersonal conflicts overlap with internal conflicts like the drivers' wish to drive and their wish for calm, clean air and nice surroundings.

Conflicts between needs result from limited resources: The decision to satisfy a need is related to opportunity costs, i.e. the possibilities for satisfying other needs become restricted by any activity.

Behaviour of individuals in such conflict situations is depicted in economic theory with the help of game theory, which analyses strategic decision situations (Osborne, 2004; Parsons, 2002; Rasmusen, 2005). The prisoner's dilemma is a well-known example of a model of game theory (Blum, 2000; Fritsch, 2005). With the help of this model it can be shown that the result of the game might be improved by incurring binding agreements or by changing the payings out of the game by superior instances.

The problem overusing the environment is described by the game theoretical model of the "tragedy of common ground": "On the common ground of a farm village, certain farmers act rationally by enlarging their flock, even if the productivity of the land decreases per piece of cattle, because the disadvantage is shared by everyone whereas the advantage favors only the farmer. Consequently, the common ground is overused in the long run and founders." (Blum, 2000, p. 394)

Applied to environmental questions, this means that, for the individual, it is most advantageous if all others act in an environmentally friendly way and only the individual himself acts selfishly. In this case, one does not have to make the effort to act in an environmentally friendly manner but, nevertheless, enjoys the advantage of low environmental pollution.

The examples of societal needs discussed in the literature can all be attributed to internal and interpersonal conflicts of needs. These are not needs which go beyond individual needs, but individual needs that are insufficiently satisfied or that are not satisfied at all due to the necessity of decisions between conflicting needs. As a result of these conflicts, the affected individuals do not have their needs met as well as possible. Game theoretical models show that institutions which change the payments of the game can improve the situation for all involved individuals. Therefore, governmental interventions are rational in order to solve conflicts of needs, if the allocative result can be improved or a distribution requested by society can be attained.[17]

[17] Market distortions like public goods are one main reason for internal and interpersonal conflicts of needs; see chapter C.1.

B.3.3 What is meant by the concept of basic needs?

The following chapter discusses which of the variable and contradictory human needs are the most important, which are the vital ones that need-oriented measures should concentrate on. The debate about the concept of basic needs was and is being carried out above all in the scope of development politics. Here, the aim is to eliminate hunger, illiteracy and environmental degradation by concentrating on the things people really need (Empacher, 2002). However, it is no simple task to find out what should be included in the concept of basic needs.

Schwefel (1978) compares the discussion of basic needs with the Rorschach test: The concept of needs plays the role of the inkblot to be interpreted during the test. Despite this rather pessimistic approach, numerous more or less comprehensive catalogues of basic needs can be found in the literature (Nuscheler, 1996; Sottoli, 1999; Streeten, 1981). Table 2 gives an overview of basic needs identified in literature.

Material basic needs
Nourishment, housing, clothing, provision of sufficient clear drinking water, sanitary facilities, health services, educational facilities, combustibles and lubricants, public transport, equipment and furniture for households, contraceptives, cultural facilities, possibilities for recreation, social security
Non-material basic needs
Satisfying employment possibilities in diversified labour markets with adequate wages, participation, political freedom, economic start-up-equity, safeguarding of basic human rights, possibilities for self-realisation as an individual and within groups, national and cultural identity, sense in living and working

Table 2: Overview of basic needs identified in literature (Nagel, 1985).

Looking at this table, it becomes obvious that basic needs cover not only physical needs. Every catalogue of basic needs will, therefore, be rather comprehensive, so that even politics oriented to basic needs must weigh and set priorities.[18]

As a result, there is no uniform recipe for a politics of basic needs. Such politics must be adapted to the respective circumstances depending on time and space. According to Eppler, the politics of basic needs in poor countries should concentrate above all on combating poverty, whereas in rich countries such a politics first requires *"a discussion about what we need most urgently and what we need less urgently*

[18] Regarding the question of which needs politics should concentrate on, the concepts of "appropriate" and "inappropriate" needs are also discussed in literature, see Hondrich, 1983; Lederer, 1979; Marcuse, 1979; Mussel, 1992.

and what we can abandon. The politics of needs requires the courage to admit to that the economic growth does not care for this. The market creates needs rather than satisfying basic needs." (Eppler, 2000, p. 102)

B.3.4 Possibilities for determining and fulfilling human needs

Needs are not outward characteristics of people. It is not possible to determine them by looking at an individual. The following methods for determining people's needs are identified in literature:

- **Surveys / Observations:** With the help of surveys, one can inquire about current wishes and opinions but cannot count on valid and reliable statements on needs, because such statements imply a high degree of concentration, consciousness and reflection (Möller, 1978). These abilities are neither evenly distributed across the population, nor are people always prepared to reflect even if they are in principle able to do so. The problem of adaptation and physical conditioning is another issue. According to the dialectical approach discussed in chapter B.3.1.3, people are both subject and object in the process of satisfying needs: They form their environment in order to satisfy their needs while simultaneously adapting their needs to the changing environment. As a result, disadvantaged people tend to adapt to the situation. They adjust their wishes and expectations to what is feasible in their opinion. Thus, conducted surveys showed that "*only those ideas, wishes and behaviour can be identified, which are marked by the restriction of existing offers and means available.*" (Lederer, 1979, p. 22) Also discussed critically in literature are wishes expressed by interviewees that cannot be realised for various reasons (Heinemann-Knoch, 1977; Hondrich, 1983; Meyer Abich, 1979).

- **Elections:** In democratic countries, elections belong to the most important mechanisms for finding out preferences. Usually, a distinction is made between representative and direct election procedures and between the different rules of voting. Models of direct democracy with the participation of all inhabitants in important far-reaching decisions are not possible in highly populated societies. This is why representative election models are used. A critical point concerning these models is that privileged groups are more represented than other social classes in the institutions elected to represent the interests of all people (Lederer, 1979). Furthermore, weighing is always necessary due to contradictions between different interests. Here, environmental concerns are often neglected. Another problem is the so-called multiple preferences, which is when voters regard more than one situation as the best.[19]

- **Migration:** Migration is a chance to reveal preferences for locally offered goods. Responsible administrations offer different quantities and qualities of these goods and levy different taxes for financing them. Mobile individuals reveal their preferences for certain local public goods by taking up residence in these places. They settle where the package of goods and taxes best suits their preferences. This mechanism of revealing preferences only functions with public goods, the usage of which is locally restricted.

- **Market mechanism:** With the help of the so-called "invisible hand" of the market (Smith, 2003), it is possible to derive needs from the demand for certain goods. The market mechanism is an appropriate instrument for the coordination and achievement of individual aims if it functions freely: Exchange processes run voluntarily and all exchanging partners try to reach their individual aims by joining the market process. The following critical aspects concerning the market mechanism are highlighted in literature:

    - Criticism of the economic behavioural model: According to the economic behavioural model, the situation in which individuals make decisions is described substantially by two elements: by the individuals' preferences and by restrictions. According to preferences, individuals consider their personally available options for acting and decide on the alternative which corresponds best to these preferences. This *"rational"* selection is also called *"benefit maximisation under side conditions with uncertainty"* (Kirchgässner, 2000, p. 14). In empirical investigations, partial deviations from this model were proven, for instance, if the probabilities of events were not correctly included in decisions or if preferences were inconsistent (Voss, 2005).

    - Market imperfection: There is a set of conditions for the problem-free functioning of offer and demand. In economics, these are summarised

[19] Multiple preferences can appear when the voters have to vote not only for one variable but for several variables summarised in one programme. E.g. transport is usually only one of many themes in election campaigns, and one which often does not have the highest priority (Wellisch, 2000).

by the term "perfect market." Examples of particular attributes of perfect markets are free market access and the homogeneity of goods traded (Blum, 2000). These perfect markets, as they are described in microeconomic theory, never exist in reality. As a result, disturbances in the interrelation of offer and demand exist, causing restrictions on the ability of the market mechanism to articulate and satisfy human needs.

- Only the material aspects of needs, i.e. needs expressed on the market, can be captured by the market mechanism; not everything that humans need is traded on the market. Examples of non-traded "goods" are rights and liberty and other intangible needs like confidence, hope, love and security. Vast ownership and the respective ability to make large payments entitle one to a corresponding consumption on the market, but a comprehensive satisfaction of needs does not necessarily result from this (Eppler, 2000). Here, needs that cannot be satisfied administratively by politics are affected. However, politics offers possibilities for supporting the satisfaction of these needs indirectly, for instance by supporting families.

- Distributional questions: Another point of criticism is whether people have effective access to the means of need satisfaction, mainly time and money. Only those who can afford to pay for it can participate in the market mechanism and meet the expense of the desired goods. Here, questions of distribution are addressed: Is the distribution of goods as it results from pure market mechanism socially desirable? Is it fair?

Hence, all the aforementioned approaches have gaps that do not mutually compensate but show similar consequences:

- Situations of current needs are described without really taking future needs into consideration.
- The interests of socially disadvantaged groups tend to remain underexposed.

In light of the above mentioned difficulties, the different methods should be applied parallelly in order to make statements about the needs of people and options for their satisfaction. Figure 7 summarises the discussed methods for determining and satisfying human needs; needs can be determined by surveys, elections and migration. For the satisfaction of needs, various instruments of governmental intervention are available. Only the market mechanism can determine as well as satisfy human needs.

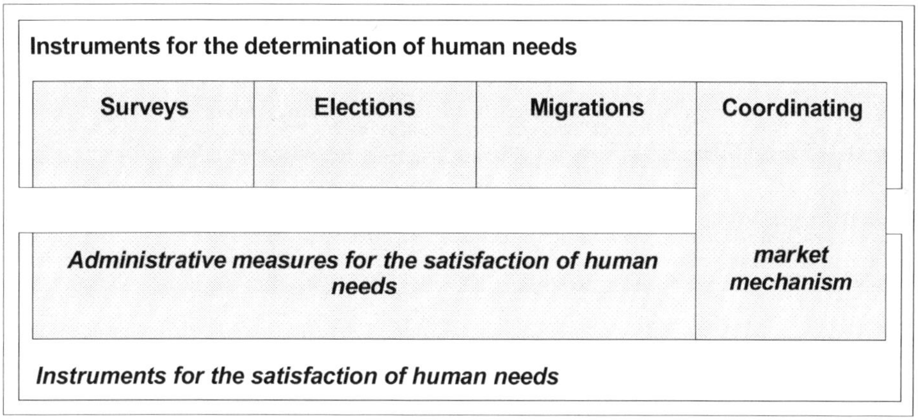

Figure 7: Means for determining and satisfying human needs.

B.4 Conclusions for concretising sustainable transportation development

B.4.1 Deductions from the need-theoretical analysis

In the following chapter, the different aspects of need research presented in the preceding chapters are brought together by discussing their significance for designing sustainable transport development.

Three theoretical views on the concept of needs were identified in chapter B.3.1: Approaches which regard needs as behavioural drive; approaches which regard needs as objective requirements and approaches of individual self-realisation which try to combine both aspects and assume a mutual influence between humans and environment.

Authors of the first direction, with Maslow as the best-known supporter, understand needs as behavioural-drive. This approach is less suitable for planning since it concentrates particularly on the explanation of internal structures and processes. Needs are regarded as human characteristics. The influence of the society on humans remains in the background. In addition, the conclusions that can be drawn are too general for concrete planning. Nevertheless, some important conclusions from the Maslow needs hierarchy can be drawn for the present work:[20]

- Human needs can only sometimes be satisfied through the consumption of goods: human affection, attention and self-realisation cannot be bought. It is not possible to satisfy these intangible needs administratively through societal planning, but it is possible to provide the conditions for satisfying them.
- Needs are changeable: They differ depending on type and stage of development of the respective society, as well as on the social status and the phase of life of people within the society.
- Needs are various and contradictory: There are conflicts both within the need systems of individuals and between the needs of different individuals. Therefore, need-associated planning must always set priorities.

Maslow's need-systematic gives an overview of the needs we have, as well as of starting points for the discussion about why the urgency of individual needs changes.

The authors mentioned in chapter B.3.1.2 have a completely different view of human needs. They understand needs as objective individual and social requirements, and thus they change the view from the assumption of motivation-guided behaviour to social standards, values and goals. This aspect is the basis for planned economic systems in particular. The task of planning consists here of arranging the different sectors of society in such a way that the social goals are achieved and humans "get" everything they "need" in order to reach the set goals.

However, it is doubtful that a comprehensive consideration of human needs is possible through such planning. The theoretical analysis showed that needs vary between individuals, that needs are in constant motion and are therefore difficult to

[20] See Brösse, 1999 for economic conclusions from the Maslow needs hierarchy.

assign and even more difficult to predict. When interpreting the term "human needs" as an objective requirement, only some of the needs can be considered.

For the present work, the third dialectic approach, presented in chapter B.3.1.3, is used as a basis. Here, influences of the first and second approach are considered. Needs are considered to be the driving force of human behaviour and become, as a result of behaviour, objective facts in the form of achieved levels of need satisfaction. The associated process of need development and need fulfillment is regarded as vital for the development of human identity and is carried out in the interplay of humans with their environment.

Humans are thereby both subjects and objects in the world surrounding them. Their integration into the process of need fulfillment is strongly needed in order to become subjects. This "becoming a subject process" takes place through the satisfaction of needs and cannot be shifted to a distant future in which humans are able to give *"their own answers"* (Marcuse, 1979, p. 26)[21] on questions about their "true" needs. Even at the risk that – judged by certain values or goals – needs can be "wrong," the formulation of the needs should not be left to experts without involving the affected individuals.

[21] See Hondrich, 1983; Lederer, 1979; Mussel, 1992 for the discussion of "true" and "wrong" needs.

The following important conclusions result from the theoretical analysis and form the basis for the following chapters:

- Instability was identified as an important characteristic of human needs. Individual needs form and change in relation to the environment: Humans shape their environment and are, themselves, shaped by their behaviour. People create new means of satisfying their needs whereby, again, new needs develop. Pros and cons from actions are weighed out under changing conditions, and by doing so individual behaviour is again and again decided anew and adapts to the changing needs.
- Needs are thereby not psychological facts or features of humans but a dynamic variable and represent a process in a specifically spatial, temporal and social context. In this context, needs can be determined objectively. In the exchange of humans with their environment, needs are subjective aspects of this exchange.
- A complete fulfillment of human needs is not possible since contradictions exist both within a person's need system and between need systems of different individuals. Need fulfillment is therefore always relative and developed equilibriums are unstable.
- Therefore, neither needs nor the degree of need satisfaction can be determined without involving the affected individuals. This corresponds to the assumption that the definition as well as the fulfillment of needs are components of individual self-realisation, and thus are necessary for the development of identity.
- Finally, the process character of sustainable transportation development can be confirmed as a result of the need-theoretical discussion. Sustainable transportation development is regarded as development oriented to human needs. A final determination of this goal is only possible for concrete application by including the affected individuals.

B.4.2 Development of task fields for sustainable transportation development

In chapter B.4.2, task fields for sustainable transportation development are established on the basis of the definitions discussed in chapters B.1 and B.2 as well as on the basis of the need-theoretical analysis in chapter B.3.

B.4.2.1 Allocative task field

Of the methods for determining and satisfying human needs presented in chapter B.3.4, only the market mechanism is able to determine and satisfy needs simultaneously. The investigation of market functionality is the object of economics. Fritsch defines the term "market" as *"all exchange processes that accrue from the meeting of offerers and demanders"* (Fritsch, 2005, p. 7). The exchange processes run voluntarily. A functioning market coordinates individual actions and decisions in such a way that no control by a central institution is required: As individuals maximise their use, balances are obtained, which are optimal from a society's viewpoint and allow the best possible satisfaction of human needs. Surveys, elections and migration as further methods for determining needs are substantially less flexible and slower to react.

These characteristics of the market mechanism are summarised in the first fundamental theorem of welfare economics which states that markets with perfect competition lead to pareto-efficient resource allocations (Stiglitz, 1996; Voss, 2005).

These assumptions of the economic behavioural model are sometimes criticised in literature by referring to empirical investigations, in which deviations from this model were proven (Diekmann, 2004; Friedman, 1996; Voss, 2005). For the present work, this discussion is of little importance, since the task here is not to explain human behaviour but to use the abilities of the market mechanism as a means for satisfying humans needs. Even if humans do not act rationally regarding a certain offer in quantity, price and quality, by acquiring more goods than they need, the market mechanism reacts nevertheless, by increasing prices in reaction to rising demand, for example.

However, criticism concerning market failures is relevant to this work. Here, cases are addressed in which the ideal exchange of supply and demand, and consequently the ability of the market mechanism to satisfy human needs, is disturbed. This concerns the model of a perfect market which serves as a standard approach in economics for analysing the functionality of markets, the assumptions of which hardly ever exist in reality (Blum, 2000).

The theory of market failure analyses effects which must be considered if the reality differs from the assumptions of the perfect market model (Fritsch, 2005). Different so-called market failures are examined and recommendations for polito-economic interventions to correct them are developed. The aim of governmental intervention is to improve the allocation obtained by the market and thus to approach the theoretically determined optimum.

The practical relevance of the welfare-economic models as a reference standard for economic policy is a matter of dispute. Their lack of reference to reality, as well as the unconsidered practical possibilities and problems of economic policy, are seen as the main reasons why these models are criticised. However, the inadequacies become less important when referring to the theory of market failure as normative theory. It is helpful to determine under which circumstances and by which means one should intervene in the market mechanism on behalf of society. The theory of market failures does not claim to be an explanatory theory that explains the way the state acts. Therefore, the theory is obviously incomplete because the players in economic policy often act differently than recommended by theory.

As a normative theory, the theory of market failure is of great importance because it nominates necessary conditions for state interventions. The extent of market failure necessary to make state intervention reasonable cannot be determined with scientific exactness. Valuing decisions are necessary to find out whether the overall welfare can be increased by state intervention. However, reasonable interventions become possible through linking the interventions of economic policy to the theoretical recommendations. With the help of market failure theory, questions of whether there are reasons for serious limitations in the functioning of certain markets or whether the market results should be corrected for distributional reasons, can be argued explicitly.

For these reasons, the following argumentation will be based on the realisations of market failure theory. The market is the most flexible mechanism for determining and satisfying human needs and should therefore be necessarily used to facilitate sustainable transportation development. To realise its abilities, the market mechanism must as much as possible approach the characteristics of a perfect market. The first task field for sustainable transportation development results from this argumentation: The goal of any activities in this first task field should be to reduce market failures. It will be known from now on as the allocative task field.

The goal of measures within the allocative task field is to support the qualities of the market mechanism for the satisfaction of human needs.

Hence, the allocative task is to be described by indicators which illustrate the extent of market failures. This indicates to what extent the functioning of the market mechanism is ensured. In the description of this task field, parallels are drawn with the equity principle from the debate on justice. This principle is characterised by the fact that the needs of individuals are considered a function of their advance payments: Anyone who can afford it can acquire the goods necessary to satisfy their needs on the market – regardless of social or other obstacle. In order to ensure this justice, the market mechanism must function – a goal that must be aimed at by measures in the allocative task field.

B.4.2.2 The distributive task field

B.4.2.2.1 Derivation of the distributive task field

Supposing the market mechanism to be a flexible instrument for determining and satisfying human needs, the question arises: Are further task fields for sustainable transportation development needed? This must be answered in the affirmative due to the lack of consideration of distribution questions by the market mechanism. Even with an optimal allocation of resources as it is aimed by the allocative task field, the satisfaction of certain needs for certain groups of people might not, in some circumstances, be ensured.[22] It is conceivable that despite good market results – measured for instance in terms of the national accounts (like the GDP) – the basic needs of certain groups of people are insufficiently satisfied due to imbalances in

[22] The distributions existing as result of market processes are exclusively orientated to the equity principle. Blum (2000) calls the sharing of the payments according to the equivalence principle one of the distribution functions of (neoclassical) competition.

the distribution of market results. This aspect of distribution is addressed in the second fundamental theorem of welfare economics. This theorem states that it is possible to reach every pareto-optimal allocation with the help of a decentralised market mechanism by varying the initial endowment with resources.[23] With the help of this fundamental theorem, it is possible to define the area of validity of welfare economics: With its help, pareto-optimal situations can be determined for given initial endowments and constraints. Whether resulting distributions are desired by society does not fall under the jurisdiction of welfare economics.[24] Therefore, the justification of distributionally motivated measures should be separated clearly from measures falling into the allocative task field.

From this argumentation, the necessity for a distributional task field for sustainable transportation development results with the goal of compensating market mechanism deficits regarding the satisfaction of human needs.[25]

The question of which of the possible efficient resource allocations should be aimed at can be answered by considering fairness: Inputs for and outputs from the market mechanism should be fairly distributed among people living today and between current and future generations. Thus, the focus of the distributive task field is on the norm "justice."[26]

Chapter B.4.2.2.2 gives a general overview of the discussion of the term "justice" and contextualises this term in the sustainable transportation development debate. On this basis, in chapters B.4.2.2.3 and B.4.2.2.4, two distributional task fields for sustainable transportation development are derived as components of the distributional task field described above.

---

23 As with the first fundamental theorem, even here the condition of perfect competition applies, see Stiglitz, 1996.

24 The so-called "pareto-optimal" measures for redistribution are an exception, see Fritsch, 2005; Wellisch, 2000.

25 This necessity of actions by the state going beyond measures to improve allocation can be derived also from the debate on justice, which shows deficits of the equity principle and recommends the parallel use of further justice principles. Distributional measures show parallels to the needs- as well as to the equal-principle: The justice of distributions is not measured by the advance payments of affected individuals, but rather by their needs; see Sen, 2000.

26 In many cases there is a trade-off between the effort to achieve efficiency and the effort to achieve justice, see Stiglitz, 1996.

B.4.2.2.2 The term "justice"

Justice is one of the oldest guidelines for the political and social behaviour of humans and is accepted as such to a large extent. However, there are different opinions as to the exact definition of the term "justice." Several sciences deal with these questions from different perspectives: philosophy, social sciences, economics and psychology (Ekardt, 2004; Litman, 2006a; Schade, 2000).

First, an important distinction is made between procedural and distributive justice. The former refers to procedures for achieving certain distributions of goods (Epp, 1998; Tschentscher, 2000; Tyler, 2000), while the latter deals with the results of the distribution process. In the debate on sustainability, the focus is on questions of distributional justice by developing criteria for the distribution of rights and obligations, natural resources, economic goods and social positions.[27] However, the importance of questions of procedural justice must not be underestimated since the implementation of distributive justice is not possible without considering procedural questions.

When dealing with theories of distributional justice, a differentiation between philosophical-normative approaches and empirical concepts must be made (Sabbagh, 2002). The subject of normative approaches is the "shall," i.e. rules are developed and justified for guiding the distribution of social goods and burdens in society. The discussion is mainly about what should be regarded as socially fair from a moral point of view, as well as which structure a society should have so that the processes of distribution run fairly.

In the empirically oriented sciences like psychology and sociology, the "be" is at the centre of discussion:

- Which distribution principles do people consider fair in which situations? What are these feelings dependent on?
- From which reasons does different distributional behaviour result?
- To what extent do humans feel unfairness in the case of unfair rewarding?
- What are the consequences of perceived unfairness?

[27] "*Sustainable development is above all a question of distribution between generations and thus a question of justice.*" (Kirchgässner, 1997, p. 20)

When investigating these questions, different influences on the sense of justice and on justice behaviour are considered, like the influences of personality, social origin, economic interests and sense of belonging to a certain cultural environment.[28]

Important normative justice concepts, mostly discussed in economic literature, are utilitarianism and the theory of the justice of John Rawls.[29] Utilitarianism was developed in the 19th century and determines the welfare of a society with the help of aggregated utility of the individual members of society (Stiglitz, 1996). Therefore, a "just" distribution is characterised by the fact that the utility sum is maximised.[30] Following this criterion, the level of justice increases when the poorest groups of society give up some of their utility and the utility of the richest groups of society increases by at least the same amount.

Apart from difficulties in measuring utility,[31] this approach can lead to extremely unequal distribution by failing to ensure the satisfaction of basic needs for all members of society. In order to consider this problem, weighted sums are often used.[32] By choosing the weights of the different individual utilities, the societal esteem of certain individuals can be expressed.

In his best-known work "A Theory of Justice" (1971), John Rawls supports the idea that the welfare of society depends only on its poorest members (Rawls, 2003). The impoverishment of the poorest society member therefore cannot be counterbalanced by any increase in the utility of richer individuals however high this may be. According to Rawls, a measure is regarded as welfare-increasing if it increases the utility of the poorest, regardless of the development of the utilities of all other members of society.[33] Rawls' welfare function is called minimax-function since it operationalises the aim of maximising the utility of the poorest members of society.

---

28 See Liebig, 2002 for the relation between normative and empirical approaches as well as for the potential for approaching both.

29 See Wellisch, 2000 for further theories of governmental activities, like the minimal state by Nozik or approaches by Buchanan and Tullock, according to which governmental activities are always justified, if all members of society agree voluntarily.

30 The aggregation of individual utilities comes with large difficulties. One restriction, which is generally imposed on the aggregation function, is that it rises with increasing utility of any individual, see Varian, 2004.

31 See Blum, 2000; Kreuzburg, 1999; Varian, 2004 for the discussion of ordinal versus cardinal measuring of utilities.

32 This form of utilitarianism was propagated by John Stuart Mill (1806-1873).

33 See Wellisch, 2000 for Rawls' argumentation of the "veil of ignorance."

Apart from these fundamental theories of justice, justice principles are used in the literature in order to formulate "fair" distribution rules by considering personal and situational conditions. These are used both in normative and in empirical approaches. Below, the most important justice principles are discussed:[34]

- Need principle: "Everyone according to their needs." The needs of each individual are considered independently of the respective advance payments, considering exclusively the neediness of the individual. This principle is used particularly in desperate situations and in cases of close personal relations between the partners, as in parent-child relations or nurse-patient relations. The goal of this principle is to compensate for discrimination resulting from inabilities caused through no fault of ones own, as in the case of physically challenged individuals. The aim is to make the satisfaction of basic needs possible for all people.

- Equality principle: "Everyone the same." Goods are evenly distributed among the interaction partners, regardless of their needs, commitment or contributions (absolute equality). This principle is used to encourage cooperation, partnership and solidarity as important conditions for things like teamwork. There is no additional information necessary for the application of the equality principle. Therefore, it is often used, if the deciding parties are under time pressure, if the communication costs are high or if the profit is low and thus the effort of further negotiations is not worth it. One point of criticism is that the equality principle can have a performance-reducing effect, since usually a prohibition of competition is connected with it.

- Equity principle: "Everyone according to their performance."[35] Profits are distributed in proportion to the advance payments (relative equality). Three main rules are used: Distribution according to (a) effort, (b) actual contribution or (c) respective ability. Unequal distributions and differentiated rewards are therefore regarded as fair and the requirement of equal chances for everybody is emphasised: Everyone is responsible for their own social progress regardless of social barriers. This principle is used particularly in economically-oriented competitive conditions and leads to high commitment and productivity due to its

[34] Some authors state further principles like the principle of justice of vested rights, according to which goods should be shared proportionally to the current possession (Diefenbacher, 2001; Grunwald, 2006; Schade, 2003a).

[35] Some authors call this principle the "contribution principle" (Druwe, 1999; Schade, 2000; Trinder, 1991).

motivating effect. Points of criticism of the equity principle are the missing of emotional bonds as well as unfavourable consequences of competitive pressure.

Each of the three principles provides special rules for the distribution of goods. The parallel use of several justice principles won out to a large extent in the justice discussion against one-dimensional approaches which mostly emphasise the equity aspect (equity principle). The universal demand of one-dimensional approaches to set up a generally valid theory of human interaction and, therefore, to supply one unique basic criterion for the evaluation of justice, could not be confirmed in empirical investigations. These investigations proved that the equity principle appears rarely as an exclusive principle in reality and that reflections on justice are also influenced by other motives like helpfulness, aspiration for power or desire for recognition (Diefenbacher, 2001; Druwe, 1999; Grunwald, 2006).

Preferences for one of the three principles depend above all on the kind of the social relationship in which the distribution takes place. To some extent, the equity and the equality principle are used in combination. The equality principle serves to secure a minimum standard; performances going beyond that minimum are considered by the equity principle.

An important characteristic of the debate on sustainability is the consideration of future generations in the justice considerations. This intergenerational aspect becomes clear in the Brundtland definition of sustainable development which refers to the needs of present and future generations. However, whether the two postulates of inter- and intragenerational justice should be considered equally in rank is controversial:[36]

- One position with regard to the Brundtland-report considers both postulates equally important from their normative claim, with intragenerational justice instrumental to intergenerational justice. A comprehensive theory of intergenerational justice with this view is developed in the study "In Fairness to Future Generations" by Brown-Weiss (1999).[37] According to this theory, each generation is entitled to use the inheritance passed on by preceding generations and is at the same time obliged to administer it in trust for the following generations.

---

[36] Radke (1999) mentions nature as third object of justice (justice to nature). See Grunwald, 2006; Kopfmüller, 2001 for the positions discussed below.

[37] Kopfmüller (2001) develops the three following rules of sustainability refering to Brown-Weiss: the securing of human existence, the preservation of social productive potential and the maintaining of options for development.

- To some degree the abolishment of the separation between inter- and intragenerational justice has been demanded. Instead, the "subject quantity" of justice considerations should be expanded to include people living in the future. The only special characteristic of intertemporal justice is that present generations have the possibility to influence the shape of further development, while future generations do not (Acker-Widmaier, 1999).
- A second position regards intra- and intergenerational justice as normative of equal standing, but assigns priority to intergenerational justice regarding analytic aspects: The rights of future generations are to be protected with highest priority. The options remaining within this framework for present generations are to be distributed evenly. The concept of "Umweltraum" is an example of operationalising this position. It describes the extent to which human use of the natural environment is possible without substantially harming it in the long term. The "Umweltraum" is determined by the ability of natural resources to be regenerated; as well as by their availability (BUND/Miserior, 1996).
- A third position regards only the intergenerational aspect as constitutive for the model of sustainable development (Birnbacher, 1996; Kastenholz, 1996; Radke, 1999). Intragenerational questions of justice should be considered as a stand-alone target area, which is in partial accord and in partial conflict with the goal of sustainability (Renn, 1996). However, some authors point out the causal relationship between intragenerational justice and the goal of sustainability. This is not constitutive for sustainable development, but is nevertheless relevant in this context (Birnbacher, 1999).

The next chapters will discuss which of the justice concepts presented above seem suitable for the following lines of argument. On this basis, two distributive task fields will be derived: the social task field and the resource task field.

B.4.2.2.3 The social task field

The most important criterion for evaluating distributions concerning sustainable development is ensuring the satisfaction of the needs of present and future generations. Against this background, the concept of utilitarianism, which evaluates distributions mainly by societal utility, is only suitable for the assessment of distributions, if the needs of the poorest social groups are weighted very highly. Otherwise the satisfaction of all people's needs is not ensured by this concept.

In order to ensure consideration of the poorest people's needs, this study concentrates on that population. Contrary to Rawls, policies for supporting sustainable development should not aim at maximising the utility of the poorest individuals, but at guaranteeing basic needs, which are to be specified for all society members by a societal discussion.

Firstly, this goal follows from the suitability of the market mechanism for the determination and satisfaction of needs. Surveys, elections and migration as further methods for determining needs are slower as well as less flexible, and should therefore only be used if the satisfaction of needs is insufficiently ensured by the market mechanism.

Secondly, the goal of satisfying basic needs for all humans follows from the Brundtland definition of sustainable development, which is used as starting point and basis for the argumentation in the present work and which refers expressly to basic needs: *"Sustainable development requires meeting the basic needs of all."* (Brundtland, 1987, p. 24) Thirdly, the goal of satisfying basic needs for all humans can be derived from the idea of the welfare state, which was shaped by Müller-Arnack and is described as follows: *"The sense of the social market economy is to connect the principle of liberty on the market with that of social reconciliation."* (Blum, 2000, p. 525)[38] Authors in economic literature also notice widespread consent in ensuring a subsistence level for all members of society (Wellisch, 2000).

These different lines of reasoning result in a second task field for sustainable transportation development: the social task field. The goal of the social task field is it to ensure the satisfaction of needs that are deemed basic. The satisfaction of these

[38] The welfare state principle is also embodied in German basic law: There (art. 20, 28 GG) the order at the state is formulated *"to order the community according to the principles of social justice."* (Blum 2000, p. 487); See also Litman: *"We need a standard definition of basic accessibility and basic mobility, which identifies 'essential' activities and ranks trips according to their importance to a community."* (Litman, 2003, p. 25).

needs should even be ensured when the advance payments necessary in the view of the equity principle cannot be provided by the affected individuals.

> The aim of the social task field is to guarantee a basic transportation supply for all people.

This goal is applied equally to present and future generations. Thus, the first of the three positions concerning the weighing of different generations' needs, presented in chapter B.4.2.2.2, is used as the basis for the following argumentation. Intra- and intergenerational justice are regarded as equally important. This position plays a decisive role in the international debate on sustainable development. Intra- and intergenerational justice are so closely related that it seems difficult, and moreover not meaningful, to separate them.

By regarding the two aspects as equally important, the question of how to deal with trade-offs must be clarified. In the present work, the hierarchy of objectives, developed by Daly in the framework of strong sustainability, is used for handling this problem.[39] This hierarchy stresses the primacy of the problem of scale within the ecological field: The alignment of consumption of natural resources to ecological carrying capacity has the highest priority. Questions of distribution and allocation of environment use have to be handled secondarily and should be bound to the determined restriction of carrying capacity, because the preservation of natural resources is vital for the survival of humankind. All further reflections on justice are superfluous if this condition is not met, and as a result the basis for existence is endangered.[40]

Here parallels between the first and second positions, discussed in chapter B.4.2.2.2, appear, because the latter stresses the priority of maintaining the ecological carrying capacity. Depending on the weighing of the different goal dimensions, an approximation between the first and the second position becomes obvious, and a differentiation between both becomes difficult and no longer meaningful. Future generations can only make use of the same rights as present generations if the natural

[39] See chapter B.1.

[40] This refers, among other things, to the rules of sustainability for protecting human existence, which were formulated by Grunwald, 2006; Kopfmüller, 2001.

conditions for this are given. Today's activities must not prevent future generations from asserting the claims resulting from the justice principles.

Therefore, for the following lines of thought equal standing of intra- and intergenerational justice is assumed. The justice principle used in the present work consequently corresponds to a large extent to the argumentation of representatives of critical sustainability.

However, the third position remains unconsidered in the following chapters, since an exclusive consideration of intergenerational justice seems neither meaningful nor feasible.

The goal of guaranteeing basic needs satisfaction concerns the distribution of the incomes obtained at the market as the most important topic of the economic distribution theory and policy. Applied to the transport sector, this means the distribution of transport offers: By granting more transport offers to certain individuals than they could afford according to the equity principle, their income is increased indirectly. *"The essence of social coexistence lies hereby in the fact that compared to competitive allocation, certain individuals can get more than they have paid for and the reverse; thus 'free rider' and 'sucker' appear."* (Blum, 2000, p. 383)

The transport sector is less responsible for the direct satisfaction of basic needs because of its service function, but more responsible for guaranteeing options for satisfying these needs. All humans should have the chance to reach destinations where the satisfaction of their basic needs is possible.

Therefore, this social aspect of sustainable transportation development is operationalised by the right to a basic transportation supply, which must be established normatively by a societal discussion. This right can be used as an exclusion criterion to prepend welfare analysis by excluding measures in advance that do not meet this criterion. The other option for operationalising this right is to make the needs of the affected groups of society a very high priority within welfare analysis.

B.4.2.2.4 The resource task field

In addition to the distribution of market results, which should be regulated within the social task field, the distribution of input factors for the economic process also requires governmental measures to supplement the market process. The task of the market mechanism is to secure the efficient use of available resources. In the context of the sustainability debate, we must ask the following questions: Which resources should be made available and how are the finite resources to be distributed intra- and intergenerationally?

Measures of distributional policy dedicated to this point of criticism are assigned to a third task field in the context of need-oriented transport development: the resource task field.

> The job of the resource task field is to regulate the distribution of production factors which are to be led by the market process to efficient use.

In the literature, the production factors work, capital and environment are distinguished.[41] For sustainable transportation development, the environmental factors above all are relevant, since here the potential for conflict is significant and shows a tendency to rise. In particular, vehicle miles travelled (VMT) have been characterised by strong growth in recent decades with the result that improvements in specific environmental impacts were overcompensated. For these reasons, this work concentrates on the production factor environment with regard to the resource task field.

> The central question of the resource task field is how natural resources as input for the supply of transport services should be distributed within one and between different generations.

As with the social task field, the question of which criteria appear suitable for evaluating the fairness of resource distributions must be clarified here. The resource task field, like the social task field, has basic needs at the centre of its argument: All

41 The production factor work is divided into executive, dispositive and explorative (research) components. The production factor capital includes all goods needed as production means for manufacturing goods. The production factor environment includes all natural components going into the production process; see Blum, 2000.

humans have to be able to satisfy their basic needs, and since humans are dependent on certain services of nature in order to survive, it is necessary to secure these essential functions of nature.[42] Technical substitutions for irreversible damages or for the exhaustion of resources are conceivable, but their availability cannot be counted on.

The need for placing limits for the consumption of natural resources results from this argument of guaranteeing fundamental natural functions: In order to give all generations the chance to meet basic needs, certain limits must not be exceeded. Here, consumption limits respective of carrying capacity are addressed depending on the kind of resource. For finite resources specifications must be made about how much of the available resources certain generations may use. For regenerative resources as well as the use of the environment as drain, carrying capacities must not be exceeded.

The goal of the resource task field is the formulation of limits for the consumption of natural resources by the transport sector.

As in the social task field, the resource task field deals with measures for supplementing the market mechanism. Here, however, it is done with the goal of limiting the consumption of natural resources to an extent which must be derived from considerations of fairness. The rules to be formulated for the intra- and intergenerational distribution of natural resources provide the limits which should not be exceeded by transport activities.

42 Acker-Widmaier (1999) identifies the following functions of nature, which should be available for every individual in order to make the satisfaction of needs possible: the production function, the function of providing living space and the contemplative function of nature; see also Holstein, 2003.

Excursus: Are the discussed environmental effects of transportation not cases of market failure, particularly in the case of external costs, the internalisation of which falls into the allocative task field? Why are the described problems concerning natural resources not solved by the internalisation of external costs?

In answering these questions, the influences of both task fields on each other become obvious. For monetising external effects as a condition for their internalisation, normative assumptions are necessary, i.e. distribution questions must be answered. Which temperature rises should the calculation of climatic costs be based on? Which critical loads are defined?

These questions are distribution questions and fall into the resource task field. Only by answering these questions can external costs like climatic costs be quantified.[43] The higher the accepted temperature rise is, the lower the costs are. The internalisation of the so monetised effects is again a task to be solved within the allocative task field.

The distributional character of the consumption of finite resources is easier to understand. Prices send shortage signals but without considering the needs of future generations, because they do not have a voice on today's resource market (Wellisch, 2000).

[43] See Becker, 2002 and chapter C.1 for the discussion of problems of uncertainty with the monetisation of external effects.

B.4.3 Joining the developed task fields into a corridor of sustainable transportation development

With the three task fields established, the basic structure of the development corridor of sustainable transportation development exists. The two distributional task fields form the lower and upper boundaries which should not be exceeded by activities in the transport sector:

- The lower boundary is formed by a basic transportation supply to be guaranteed within the social task field. This should not be fallen below.
- The carrying capacity limits, to be formulated in the resource task field, form the upper boundary of the corridor and should not be exceeded.

Within the resulting development corridor, there is space remaining for the initially addressed “learning, searching and shaping,” understood to be free choice of transport activities as well as of transport offerings. The rules for all activities within the boundaries are given by the allocative task field, the goal of which is to guarantee functioning market mechanisms.

The foundation of the resulting corridor of sustainable transportation development is formed by participation: The discussion of human needs in chapter 2.1 has shown that the implementation of transport development oriented to the needs of people is not possible without involving those affected. This necessity for the participation of the affected people holds true for all three task fields and can be justified in particular by the changeable and contradictory nature of human needs. Questions of acceptance are at the foreground in the allocative and in the resource task fields. In the social task field, the cooperation of the affected people is crucial in order to achieve a good correspondence between the basic transportation supply and the existing needs of the affected people.

Figure 8 summarises the logic for the derivation of the task fields. In the following chapters, the task fields are referred to as the allocative task field, the social task field and the resource task field, by always keeping in mind that the two latter are distributional task fields for sustainable transportation development.

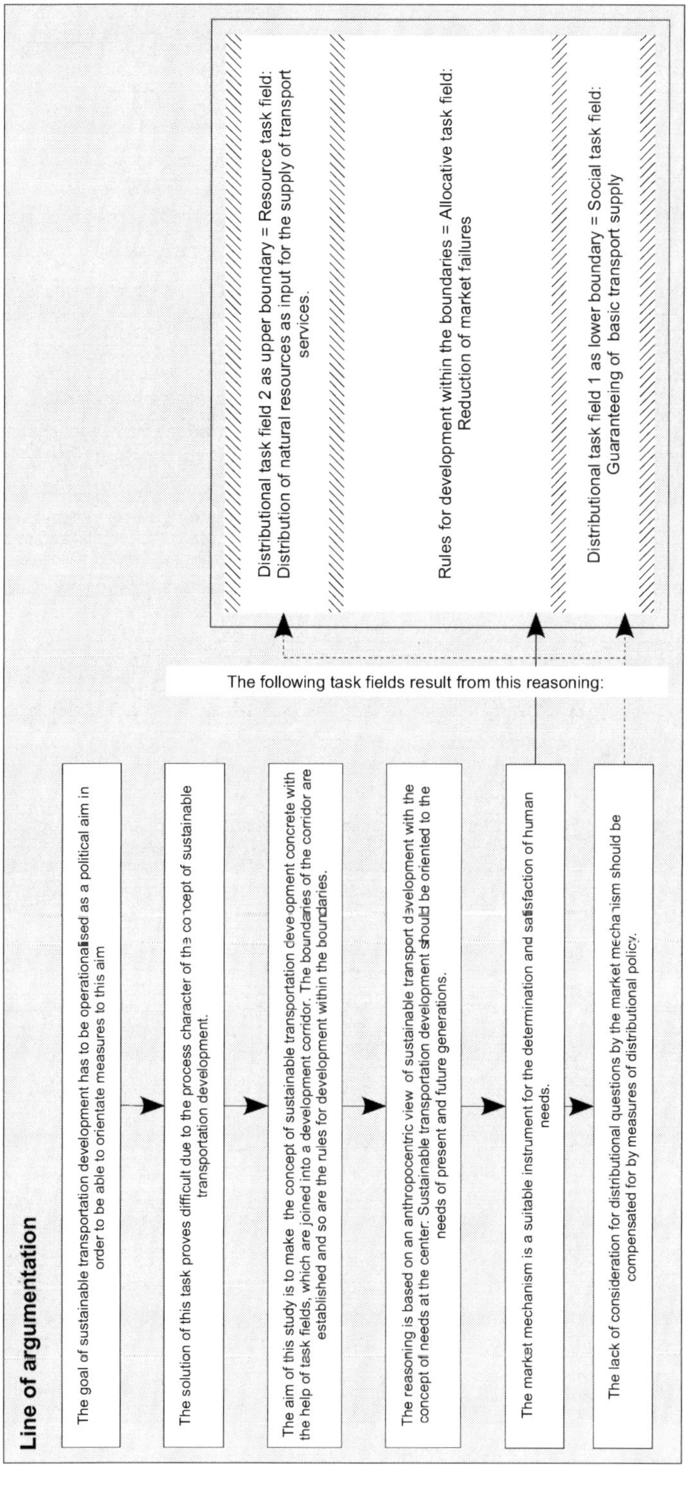

Figure 8: Line of argumentation for deriving task fields for sustainable transportation development.

C Options for concretising the development corridor

The next step is to identify options for putting the development corridor into concrete terms. This is a highly normative task that can only be done within a societal discussion. Science can provide information about suitable criteria. Figure 9 illustrates the tasks of part C: Options for making the task fields established in part B concrete components of the development corridor are highlighted, and recommendations for measures to encourage sustainable transportation development are made. Thus, the following part deals in particular with questions of method by developing possible criteria for describing the task fields.[44]

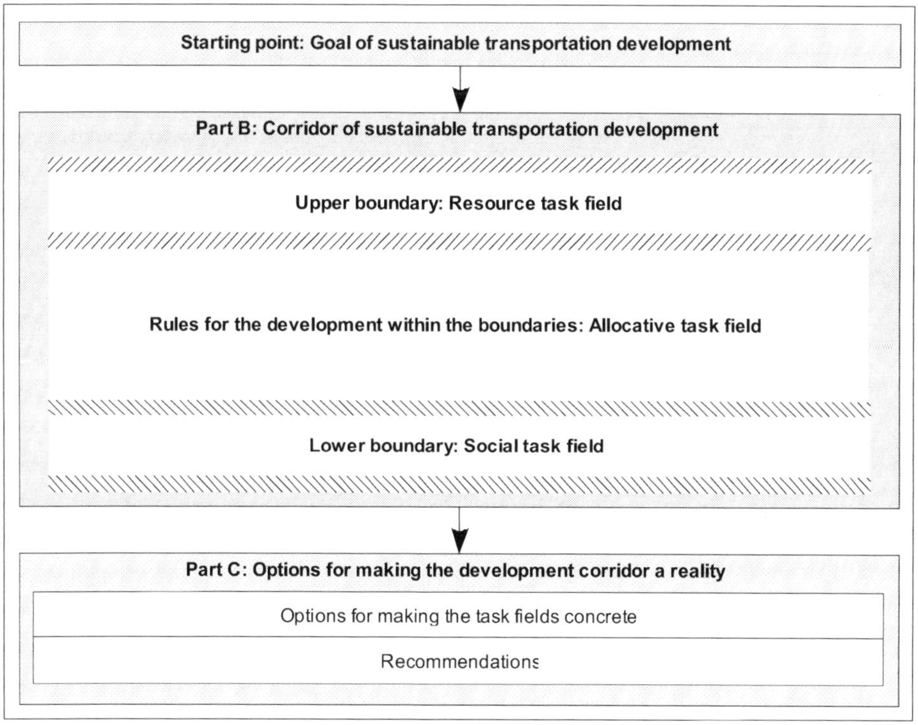

Figure 9: Overview of the steps of the study – Part C.

[44] See Gerike, 2005 for the empirical analysis, i.e. for the analysis of exemplary indicators for the allocative and the resource task fields.

The emphasis of part C lies on the social task field, in which important methodological gaps can be identified: Which criteria are suitable for operationalising a basic transportation supply? Which target figures should be formulated for the criteria? How can the different criteria describing the basic transportation supply be aggregated? Only by answering these questions can implementation deficits in this field be highlighted and measures for reducing the deficits be realised.

However, the tasks in the allocative task field are methodically relatively clear and discussed in economic literature. In this task field, the need for action, above all, can be seen, so that here the focus must be placed on the empirical part of work (Gerike, 2005). In the present work the economic foundations are briefly discussed in chapter C.1.1. On this basis, suggestions for indicators describing the allocative task field are compiled in chapter C.1.2.

The resource task field is also characterised in particular by implementation deficits. Recommendations from a scientific point of view exist, though the realisation of these is tackled only rudimentarily. The subject of the resource task field is intra- and intergenerational distribution questions of natural resources: How can a fair distribution of these resources be arranged? This question is discussed in chapter C.3.

The structure of part C necessarily reflects the task fields established in part B. Options for concretising the task fields are discussed, with each task field corresponding to one chapter.

Finally, in chapter C.4, recommendations are developed. In chapter C.5 the consequences of using the development corridor for the assessment of measures are shown.

C.1 The allocative task field

As a result of chapter B.4.2.1, the allocative task field deals with measures for correcting the market mechanism in order to optimally use its ability for the articulation and satisfaction of needs.

Chapter C.1.1 discusses which market failures are referred to in the transport sector for justifying state intervention, which measures are suitable to correct market failures and which measures are used at present. Based on this, chapter C.1.2 discusses possible indicators for describing this task field.

C.1.1 Market failures as justification for state intervention in the transport sector

The questions of why no functioning markets exist in the transport sector, and what should be done in order to approach to functioning markets, are discussed in economic literature (Blum, 2000; Köberlein, 1997; Litman, 2006b; Van Suntum, 1986). Aberle (2003) categorises the justifications for state intervention in the transport sector as follows:

- Economic reasons with normative-theoretical and positive-theoretical approaches
- Political justifications

Both directions are briefly presented below.

C.1.1.1 Economic justifications

The normative-theoretical approach offers the following points as justification for state intervention in the transport sector:

- Tendency of transport markets towards ruinous competition
- Existence of natural monopolies

- Distortion of competition caused by external effects
- Characterisation of transport infrastructure as public good[45]

The first point, ruinous competition, is defined as a particularly intensive form of competition, mostly in the form of price undercutting, which leads to inefficiency. It is the result of insufficient capacity adoption, which is caused mainly by low variable costs.[46] An example of this is the inland waterway transport. The following reasons are given for the existing tendency toward ruinous competition: high fix costs, personal relationship of the skippers to their occupation and the varying, incalculable demand. State interventions like demolition actions or minimum prices for reducing overcapacity try to reduce inefficiency caused by such ruinous competition.

One can argue that there are comparable problems in other sectors of society[47] and, moreover, that there is inefficiency resulting from state interventions. Minimum prices can lead, for instance, to an increase in capacity since the guaranteed prices promise safe incomes. The result of demolition actions may be a renewal of the ships which could potentially lead to an overcompensation for the reduction in capacity.

Natural monopolies, the second case of competition failure, arise if one offerer can satisfy the demand through lower costs than two or more offerers.[48] Net monopolies supplying electricity, water or gas as well as the rail infrastructure, including stations or airports, are examples of this. Even in the case of natural monopolies, free market solutions can be found by handing over the building, financing and operation of the concerned facilities to private enterprises. Then only the responsibilities of planning the infrastructure, the supervision of the user fees and the guarantee of a discrimination-free access to the market remain at the state level. Private enterprises can participate in the planning process, and even private initiatives are con-

45 Fritsch (2005) uses the more general categories of market failures: external effects, indivisibilities, lack of information and adaption. The more specific categories listed above can be integrated into this systematics. In the present work, the more specific categories are used, because they represent the most important market failures in the transport sector and are typical for the discussion of transport problems (Stiglitz, 1996; Wellisch, 2000).

46 This form of ruinous competition has to be distinguished from ruinous competition as a strategy of powerful offerers or demanders to push smaller competitors from the market. This form of ruinous competition is not limited to the transport sector and is to be observed by the responsible anti-trust commission (Aberle, 2003).

47 Tourism e.g. is also concerned with strongly fluctuating seasonal demand.

48 That is the case with strictly monotonic decreasing average costs in the relevant area of demand (Blum, 2000; Quinet, 2004).

ceivable. The task of the state in this case would be to prove and to guarantee the compatibility of proposals with the applicable law, with competition (including between transport means), with the interests of third parties and with the superior goals of spatial and transport policy (Van Suntum, 1986; Wieland, 2001).

The third point is external costs.[49] They are a main reason for distortion in competition in the transport sector. The costs of transport-caused environmental pollution, noise, etc. are not borne by the transport users themselves, but are transferred to society as a whole, to other regions or to future generations (Gerike, 2005). To reduce external costs, it is most favourable from the economic viewpoint to charge users all costs they cause according to the polluter-pays-principle. Another currently practiced option is to support public transport as a transport means with smaller external costs than private transport – with the goal of equal treatment in competition. This is known as the second best solution. From an economic viewpoint, the internalisation of external costs as the first best solution is preferred.

The practical implementation of such a theoretically complete internalisation is problematic due to problems of information and acceptance. Marginal external costs vary heavily depending on the cost component, for instance, and on the time and region where the external cost component is caused. Prices would have to be strongly differentiated, which would result in complicated price systems. The implementation of such systems is expensive and the acceptance is low. Thus, pragmatic approximation solutions are suitable. Through them at least a tendentious decrease of inefficiency can be achieved. Measures under discussion are the standard-price-approach, license markets for reducing the environmental damages of transport and road pricing for managing problems of traffic congestion (Proost, 2004; Ricci, 2005; Wieland, 2001).

One frequently stated argument to justify the offer of transport infrastructure by the state is to regard transport infrastructure as a public good. However, the central characteristics of non-rivalry and non-excludability must be critically examined. Non-rivalry in consumption is only given as long as no overcrowding arises. Today this is rather seldom the case with the tendentiously overloaded road system, meaning that added demanders cause substantial additional costs (mainly in the form of time delays) or that widening capacity becomes necessary.

---

[49] See Baumol (1995) for an introduction into the theoretical background of external costs.

Non-excludability also has to be put into perspective in terms of advancing technical development, because the technological possibilities for causer-fair charging of infrastructure costs are becoming better and better.[50] The literature addresses different degrees of public good: Transport infrastructure definitely has characteristics of public good, but the description as specific public good must be critically examined (Aberle, 2003).

Representatives of the positive-theoretical approach refer less to the mechanisms inherent in the market for justifying state interventions, and more to the relationship between offerers and demanders on markets regulated by the state. Private offerers develop, for instance, a demand for regulation if they profit from the restrictions on trade. As a result, increasing harmonies of interest arise between the regulating and the regulated. The national supervisory authorities are engaged in confirming their right to exist. The regulated institutions, like the state-apportioned road freight trade, benefit from the reduced intensity of competition that secures their profits and hinders access to the market for new competitors.[51]

C.1.1.2 Political justifications

The political justifications for state interventions in transport markets refer mainly to tasks of public interest, i.e. the offer of transport services which are desirable and meaningful from the view of the society as a whole, but unprofitable from the business perspective. It is also referred to the welfare state principle for justifying aims of regional planning and of social policy related to specific individuals.

An example of the first aspect is public transport tracks in thinly populated areas which are unprofitable from business perspective, but which are maintained in order to grant access to social life to people without private motorisation. Measures within the range of personal social policy include social tariffs in public transport for certain person groups like pupils, pensioners and handicapped people.

Measures in this field do not aim at reducing market failures for improving the ability of the market mechanism to articulate and satisfy human needs which would be

[50] This does not mean that the problem of determing and assigning infrastructure costs is not still relevant. See DIW, 2000; Link, 2005 for the discussion of problems of calculating infrastructure costs.

[51] These questions are discussed in political economics (Buchanan, 2001; Niskanen, 2003; Persson, 2000).

relevant for the allocative task field. Political justifications concern normatively justified goals, which cannot be justified only by economic reasons and therefore are to be dealt with in the social task field discussed in chapter C.2.

C.1.2 Discussion of criteria for the allocative task field

Indicators for the evaluation of the economy focus particularly on market results. Examples are the gross national product and variables of the total national account (Constanza, 2001). However, criteria for the present work should reflect above all how well the market mechanism works.

To this end, it can be concluded from the preceding chapters that the market mechanism in the transport sector should be supported as far as possible from the economic viewpoint in order to be able to use its suitability for the articulation and satisfaction of needs. Above all, it should be deregulated.

In Germany there is still rather too much regulation, despite the processes of deregulation started in the 1980's.[52] Measures are implemented, for instance, to influence capacity by setting rules for market access for offerers of transport services or by regulating pricing on transport markets.

The goal of deregulation applies to the field of ruinous competition as well as to natural monopolies, which are the first points for the justification of state interventions in the transport sector.

Distortion of competition is a further point for justifying state interventions. Conceivable indicators for describing competition intensity on transport markets are the number and size of transport enterprises in public transport, the number of tendering procedures, the number and/or volume of quotas in freight transport and the number of minimum prices. External costs are another important indicator for describing distortions of competition. The goal should be to internalise the external costs to the greatest extent.

Neither societal tasks nor the characterisation of transport infrastructure as public good are relevant for the allocative task field, since neither concerns market failures, but rather the normative, socially desired additions of the market results.

[52] Aberle (2003) gives an overview of instruments of regulatory policy which are used for regulation in the European transport sector; see also van Suntum, 1986; Laaser, 1991.

Therefore, in the present work these points fall into the social task field with the goal of guaranteeing a basic transportation supply. Options for concretising this task field will be shown in chapter C.2.

For the following reasons, the indicator of external costs may serve as a key indicator for the allocative task field:

- The extent of external costs is very important for incentive setting by the market, since the market mechanism can only unfold its qualities for need satisfaction if the prices send the correct signals, and the market participants are therefore able to weigh costs and benefits correctly against each other.
- The problems concerning external costs are serious and urgent, but steps for their internalisation are being undertaken rather reluctantly so far.
- By internalising external effects, reductions in all environmental damage caused by transport can be achieved: The vehicle miles travelled by motorised road transport decrease, the state of public transport is strengthened, neighbourhood activities take on more weight. Thus, charging external costs according to the polluter-pays-principle has various effects – including effects on the social and resource task fields.[53]
- In the debate on sustainability, external costs are also often used as indicators for economic aspects by emphasising the importance of internalising external costs. This is referred to as a necessary, but not sufficient condition for sustainable development (Grunwald, 2006; Heiland, 2003; Rompuy, 2003; UBA, 2002).
- The indicator of external costs constitutes a well-known monetary measure for the different environmental effects of transportation. Therefore, it can be easily and well communicated.
- The determination of the external costs of transportation can be done with justifiable effort. The methodology for monetising the environmental impacts of transport is scientifically well established (Gudmundsson, 2004; Infras/IWW, 2004; Jeon, 2005; Nash, 2003). Problems concerning environmental impacts, the monetisation of which is critical, can be limited by the indication of lower bounds or ranges.

[53] Parallels to the butterfly effect, which is discussed in chaos theory, can be seen (Chen, 2003).

External costs are therefore recommended as the key criterion for the allocative task field in order to reflect the operating functionality of market mechanisms in the transport sector. The causer-fair charging of external costs is set as the goal of the allocative task field.

C.2 The social task field

C.2.1 Approach

The guarantee of a basic transportation supply was established as the goal of state interventions in the social task field in chapter B.4.2.2.3. Which requirements should such a basic transportation supply meet? Who should reach which destinations under which conditions? The answer to these questions is often argued with the concept of basic needs, the exact definition of which is, however, difficult to determine.

For this work a pragmatic and in this first step general approach is chosen by using the term "basic existence functions" to specify the concept of basic needs. Thus, the basic transportation supply is concretised in this first step by the term "basic existence functions" (ARL, 2005; Brösse, 1982; Enquete, 2000). This approach is widely-accepted in German spatial planning.

The term "basic existence functions" must be defined further in order to make it usable in describing a basic transportation supply. This definition is the task of the following chapter.

The term "basic existence functions" can be attributed to Partzsch (1966), who states seven basic existence functions:

- Shelter
- Work
- Access to provisions
- Access to education
- Access to recreation

- Access to transport
- Communication[54]

In a departure from this approach, here transport is not regarded as an independent basic existence function, but as a necessary activity to make the basic existence functions possible. This is justified by the fact that basic existence functions are described as basic needs in the present work. Transport is not regarded as a need in and of itself, but rather as a means for the satisfaction of needs.[55] Transport is referred to as a secondary need because of this characteristic.

Therefore, the goal of guaranteeing a basic transportation supply should be to facilitate activities related to the basic existence functions for all people.

In this first step, the goal of guaranteeing a basic transportation supply can be formulated as follows: All people should have shelter, should be able to work, communicate, provide for themselves, become educated and recreate.

At this stage, the goal of a basic transportation supply is still very generally formulated. The advantage of this is that it is considerably easier to reach a societal consent for a generally formulated goal than for a concrete goal. However, such qualitative goals are not suitable for planning.[56]

Therefore, the basic existence functions are broken down in the next step into sub-goals, with the help of a hierarchy of objectives. These sub-goals are concretely formulated so that they can serve as the basis of transport planning. The task at hand is thus to establish the third and possibly fourth levels of the hierarchy of objectives presented in Figure 10, thereby filling the boxes labelled with a question mark with concrete sub-goals and indicators.

[54] The basic existence function "access to provisions" is sometimes complemented by "disposing" and the basic existence function "access to recreation" by the function of "designing spare-time." Some authors suggest the function of self-defense as the 8th basic existence function (ARL, 2005; Brösse, 1982). These basic existence functions correspond well with the origin-destinations-groups used in transport planning (Schnabel, 1997, Vol. II).

[55] Exceptions like walks are not given any attention here.

[56] See Nill, 2002 for the discussion of concrete versus vague goals.

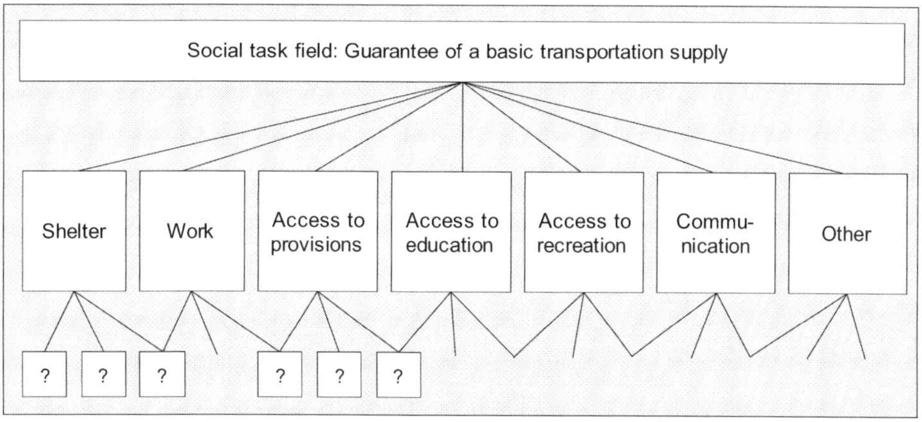

Figure 10: Operationalisation of the goal of a basic transportation supply with the help of basic existence functions.

Standards or bench marks are suitable for describing the lower levels of the hierarchy. The biggest problem in defining those standards is to determine the appropriate degree of detail.

In chapter B.3 the diversity, instability and contradictory nature of human needs were established as important characteristics of human needs. These characteristics apply also to a certain degree to basic needs. Consequently, the tasks to be dealt with to guarantee a basic transportation supply have such different characteristics that it seems neither possible nor meaningful to capture them by concrete uniform standards. The number of these standards would have to be so large that neither their determination nor the implementation would be possible at reasonable cost. Additionally, the problems in this field are so different, and in such constant change, that it seems doubtful that it is possible to develop a standard system – extensive though it might be – that would cover all basic needs.

However, a concrete definition of the reference values is necessary in order to make the basic transportation supply measurable. Reference values[57] that are too generally formulated lead to the question of whether there are any humans for whom such a basic transportation supply is not fulfilled. Transport is vital in a society like ours which is based on the division of labour. Therefore, humans organise their lives in such a way that they can do the things which they regard as important. In rural areas with poor accessibility, for instance, the Modal-Split percentage of motorised individual transport is very high. This is vital in order to deal with the natu-

[57] Just as employed individuals should be able to go to work, children should be able to go to school, etc.

rally great distances. People without an available car choose their living place in urban areas with shorter distances and better public transport supply.

Can we conclude from this example that the goal of basic transportation supply is fulfilled and that the focus should be on the reduction of cost and effort in realising the basic existence functions?[58] On a total societal level, this question may be affirmed. Looking at the local level or at particular individuals and groups of people it becomes clear, however, that there are definitely cases in which a basic transportation supply is only at times ensured. Children are a good example of this. In cities there are not enough open spaces like playgrounds. In rural areas children are dependent on their parents for most transportation, since the distances are either too far or too dangerous. The children affected by these circumstances can only access education and recreate on their own in a limited fashion.[59]

How can this contradiction be solved in order to develop a feasible and fundable standard system which addresses small-scale problems at reasonable expense?

At any rate, the determination of minimum standards, which form the first pillar of a basic transportation supply, is possible. Not every detail or issue can be covered by such standards, but illustrating important aspects of the accessibility situation of a particular area is possible. Goals in the social task field, going beyond this, can be considered by the open organisation of the standard system so that it permits case-specific extensions. Therefore, case-specific extensions form a second pillar of the basic transportation supply to be provided within the social task field.

The utility of standards or reference values is a matter of debate in literature. Fixed standards are rigid and therefore become outdated easily. Furthermore, it is difficult to find consensus about the selection of indicators, especially where quantitative target values are concerned. If such values are set too high for the own area of responsibility and are not achieved despite great effort, then criticism results. Or simply no attention is paid to the goals which have been set too high and unrealistically, since there is no chance of reaching them. If the values are set too low and are easily reached, then there is the danger that the budget for the affected depart-

58 Here the duty of public authorities to provide their services efficiently is adressed: A determined basic transportation supply should be provided at minimal costs; for the principle of rationality see Blum, 2000.

59 For further examples of deficiencies in the neighbourhood for children see Lenz, 2000.

ments will be reduced. In this case there is also the danger of neglecting the standards, if they can be met without special effort.

Among the advantages of standards, there is the possibility to compare different areas and to determine degrees of goal achievement. If goals are formulated vaguely, then it is not clear on the one hand with which measures the goal can be achieved, and whether, on the other hand, one approaches the aim through realised measures or not.

These are the crucial points argued for using concrete minimum standards to describe the basic transportation supply. This goal remains an empty phrase if it is not made concrete. The guarantee of accessibility for satisfying basic needs is always related to cost and effort, and society must decide the scale of this cost and effort. "How much" basic transportation supply should each individual be entitled to? This question can only be answered through concrete quantitative standards.

Several of the previously addressed points of criticism concerning standards can be solved by the use of minimum standards, the goal of which is not an optimal, but a "satisfying" situation. Extensions of a basic transportation supply defined in such a way are possible at any time and can be realised by the respective responsible institutions. By such a combination of fixed minimum standards and local extensions, current developments can be considered and the differences between various regions can be taken into account. Therefore, the system of minimum standards outlined in the following will serve as a stable and generally valid basis, which can be expanded by local goals. Nevertheless, finding a consensus for such a system can be difficult for the aforementioned reasons. This problem can only be solved through the common effort of all involved people.

Therefore, the intensive involvement of people is vital for the development of both pillars: the minimum standards as well as the local extensions. Only by involving the people one can concretise the basic existence functions and determine transport services which are best suited to satisfying the determined basic human needs. In this way the goals at the lowest level of the hierarchy of objectives (shown in Figure 10 on page 71) can be derived in order to operationalise the term of a basic transportation supply for concrete application. By "concrete application" certain municipalities will be meant in most cases, since they are the lowest level of spatial planning.[60]

Two necessary components of a basic transportation supply become clear:

- minimum standards as the basis
- local supplements for the final set-up of the social task field

The participation of the affected individuals is essential both for minimum standards and local supplements; it is the foundation on which a basic transportation supply can be established. Or, as pictured in Figure 11, participation is the ship which can carry a basic transportation supply.

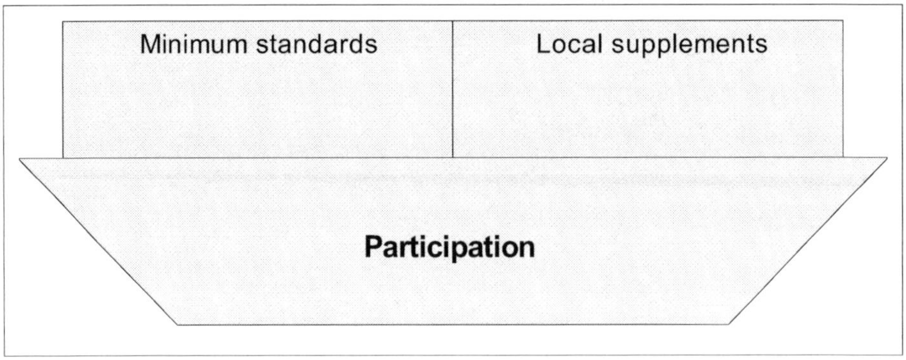

Figure 11: Components of a basic transportation supply, part I.[61]

[60] See ARL, 2005; Gerike, 2005 for the different levels of spatial planning in Germany.

[61] This depiction in Figure 11 will be used repeatedly in the coming chapters by fanning out the components as a result of the respective steps of work; see Figure 14 on page 92 and Figure 15 on page 94.

C.2.2 Transport and spatial planning components for a basic transportation supply

Figure 12 gives an overview of the structure of the following chapters as results from the chosen approach. The developed dimensions of a basic transportation supply are discussed and options are established for concretising the social task field according to the developed framework.

The subject of chapter C.2.2 is the determination of transport and spatial planning components. Both are part of minimum standards and of local supplements and therefore are treated in a common chapter. The first step in describing these components is to determine a target criterion: For which of the terms defined in chapter B.2 should minimum standards and local supplements be formulated? This question is discussed in chapter C.2.2.1.

The target criterion determined in chapter C.2.2.1 is still too general and will be concretised further in chapter C.2.2.2, where possible transport and spatial planning components of a basic transportation supply are established. This discussion is based on the developed target criterion in chapter C.2.2.1, on the definitions of transport terms in chapter B.2, and on the research of current measures and frameworks of spatial and transport policy in Germany (Gerike, 2005). It is very important to consider all this input because the basic transportation supply to be developed in the present work must fit into the existing framework in order to minimise its implementation costs.

The subject of chapter C.2.3 is participation, which will be identified as the basis of the social task field. In this chapter options for the process of organising a basic transportation supply are described.

Finally, in chapter C.2.4, possible criteria for all components of the social task field are derived.

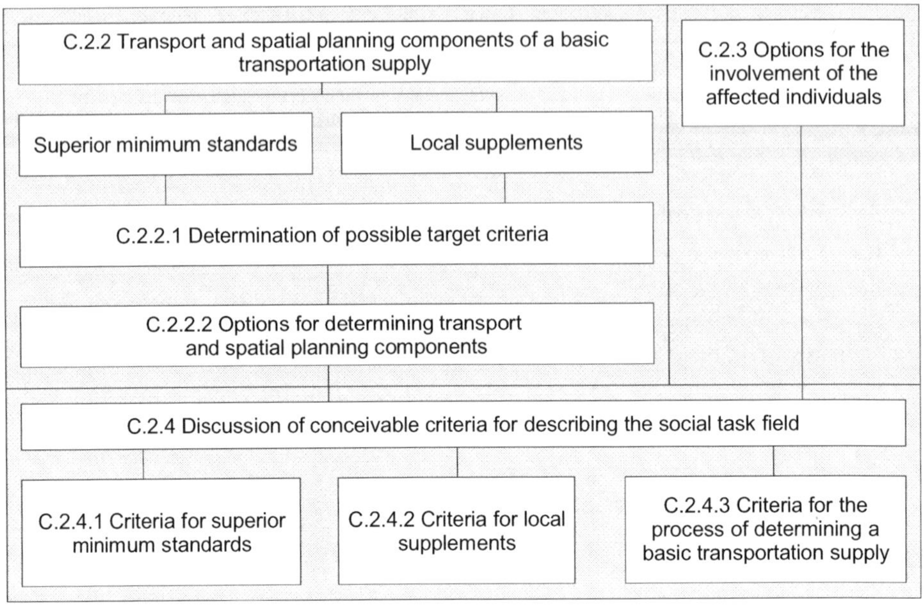

Figure 12: Structure of chapter C.2.

C.2.2.1 Discussion of possible target criteria: access, accessibility, mobility, transport and provision standards

The task of the following chapter is to address for which of the transport terms defined in chapter B.2 minimum standards and respective local supplements should be formulated.

The starting point for this discussion is the goal of a basic transportation supply established in chapter B.4.2.2: In the social task field the task of transport is to facilitate basic human needs. According to the definitions developed in chapter B.2, this goal refers to all discussed transport terms. Leaving open as many options as possible to the people means guaranteeing good accessibility to destinations relevant to the people. How people use the available possibilities is described by the term "access." Mobility and transport cover all characteristics of movement and the transport system that facilitate movement. On which of these terms should the transport and spatial-planning components to be determined within the social task field focus?

The first step to answering this question is found in the basic existence functions used in the present work. That is, as stated in chapter C.2.1, all people should have shelter, should be able to work, to communicate, to provide for themselves and to recreate.

For the fulfilment of these needs, two conditions must be met:

- The destinations necessary for the realisation of the basic existence functions must exist in reasonable quality and quantity. Here, questions of spatial planning are addressed.
- The existing destinations must be accessible to people. Here, transport offers above all are addressed.

Looking at the systematic of the transport terms developed in chapter B.2, it becomes clear that the term "accessibility" can best describe the formulated requirements. Accessibility has been defined as number and kind of reachable activities. It covers spatial planning as well as transport components. It can be objectively measured and is therefore suitable for operationalising a basic transportation supply.

The necessity of having objectively measurable target criteria applies particularly to superior minimum standards. Subjective assessments of objective offers should enter the determination of the standards by including the affected individuals in the determination of a basic transportation supply. This is necessary in order to be able to match the offers with the respective preferences. Such involvement is vital for establishing minimum standards as well as local supplements. The standards resulting from these participation processes must be objectively measurable in order to be able realise ex-ante and ex-post evaluations of measures and situations.

Specific requirements of certain groups of people may be considered by relating the components of the basic transportation supply to the affected individuals: What accessibility should be guaranteed for which individual? Who should be able to realise which basic existence functions under which conditions?

At this point the claim of the public authority to use the available means efficiently must not be left unconsidered: If the offers held remain unused, the planning misses its purpose. Means are wasted, and we must ask whether the means used would have yielded more benefit elsewhere. Therefore, the use of access indicators for the assessment of measures to implement a basic transportation supply is vital. There will always be different ways to ensure the determined accessibility, but how can the satisfaction of basic needs be facilitated at minimum expenditure? How can a maximum benefit be achieved by the accessibility to be provided within the social task field? The goal should be to reach as good a fit as possible between offer and demand.

Another aspect of efficiency is represented by the terms mobility, traffic and transport. These terms stand for the cost and effort necessary for realising activities. Reducing transport is an important goal – but it is nevertheless a second-order, supplementary goal, since transport is not a goal in and of itself. It is the means to facilitate the movement of people between relevant destinations and thus the realisation of the activities necessary for the satisfaction of their needs. Therefore, transport indicators are not suitable for describing the degree of need satisfaction. The central task of measures in the field of the basic transportation supply, and thus of the standards to be developed here, should always be the options of people, i.e. the term accessibility.[62]

From the discussion of possible target criteria, we can conclude that the term "accessibility" is central for the description of a basic transportation supply. Transport and spatial planning components should describe options for humans to arrive at the places where they can realise the activities necessary for the satisfaction of their basic needs. Therefore, accessibility is used as the target criterion for the basic transportation supply to be concretised in the following chapters.

Supplementing the accessibility indicators, access indicators and transport indicators are necessary for measuring the efficiency of the offers held in the context of the social task field. Access indicators describe the use of offers; transport indicators stand for the cost and effort that is necessary for the satisfaction of basic needs.

In the literature, simple accessibility measures from distance indicators and complex measures like utility indicators are distinguished (Gerike, 2005). For the following reasons, simple measures seem to be the most suitable for the transport and spatial planning components of a basic transportation supply. The goal of the social task field is it to make the satisfaction of basic needs possible for all people. In or-

[62] See Banister, 1994; Holz-Rau, 2006; Keller, 2002 for the discussion of the goal "higher access with less transport."

der to meet this requirement, the indicators need not illustrate the accessibility situation in the investigation area in-depth, but should be determinable area-wide at reasonable cost and effort and should be easily communicable.

In the following chapters, simple accessibility measures are used for the description of the basic transportation supply. In most cases, these are variants of the gravitation approach.[63]

C.2.2.2 Transport and spatial planning components

As a result of the discussion in the preceding chapter, C.2.2.1, the target criterion of minimum standards should be accessibility, which can be influenced essentially by two closely linked options:

- Measures within the transport sector reduce the spatial resistance between relevant destinations.
- The second option for influencing accessibility is spatial planning, which influences the spatial distribution of infrastructure facilities. Accessibility also improves when the transport conditions remain unchanged, but the distances to relevant destinations are reduced.

Both options must absolutely be considered in order to achieve good accessibility. Therefore, in the following chapters C.2.2.2.1 and C.2.2.2.2, both components are discussed separately before joining them in chapter C.2.4, in which criteria for minimum standards and local supplements will be developed, both including transport and spatial planning components.

An important requirement for developing the basic transportation supply is to fit it into existing structures and regulations of transport and spatial planning as well as possible. This makes implementation possible at reasonable expenditure.

[63] The gravitation approach calculates transport volumes in an analogy to the law of gravitaion of physiscs: Two masses gravitate towards one another dependent on their masses and distance (see Gerike, 2005; Schnabel, 1997).

C.2.2.2.1 Spatial planning components

A suitable basis for the spatial planning part of minimum standards is the central-place system, as it exists in the federal-level spatial planning of Germany. It is determined in more detail in the subordinate planning levels. In the spatial structure plan[64] of Saxony, different centres are named for the Free State of Saxony: upper, middle and lower centres (Freistaat Sachsen, 1994, 2003a). These are each responsible for their respective hinterland. Additionally, small centres as the lowest level of the Saxon system of central places are stated in the plans of Saxony's five planning regions. The catalogue of facilities listed in the spatial structure plan of Saxony is binding for the subordinate planning levels and contains detailed data on the facilities to be provided within the central towns of the different levels.[65] This catalogue was compiled by considering the different catchment areas of the facilities and is therefore a good basis for the minimum supply.[66]

Critical points concerning the central-place system are discussed in particular in the literature of spatial science, in the case of Germany in publications from the Academy for Spatial Research and Planning (ARL) (ARL, 2005; Blotevogel, 2002; Danielzyk, 2001; Turowski, 2002). One critical point is the sense of normative structuring of regions, since in many cases the transport flow does not correspond to the system of the normatively-fixed central places. Nevertheless, the central-place system is a suitable and important component of the basic transportation supply to be developed in the present work, because here transport planning is not addressed as a reaction to current developments. The task is rather to actively influence the spatial structure and the transport system with the goal of providing the possibility for the satisfaction of basic needs for all people.

The neighbourhood is of central importance when providing a basic transportation supply. This is the reason why the present central-place system is not sufficient for describing such a basic transportation supply. The distances between the small centres, the lowest level of the hierarchy, are too large (particularly in rural areas) to set standards for a neighbourhood supply.

---

64 See ARL, 2005; Turowski, 2002 for a description of the spatial structure plans as part of German spatial planning.

65 The catalogue of facilities is to be found in the appendix of the spatial structure plan of Saxony (see Freistaat Sachsen, 1994, appendix 1), see chapter E.2 for a translation of the catalogue of facilities.

66 Albrecht (1977) operationalises the different catchment areas by assigning ranking numbers to the facilities; see also Bahlburg, 1979; Borchard, 1974; Müller, 1999.

Because there are numerous (mobility) needs in this field, an extension of the central-place system by one further category is suggested. The following levels of centrality result as the basis for a conceivable system of minimum standards:

- Category I: Basic Centre
- Category II: Small Centre
- Category III: Lower Centre
- Category IV: Middle Centre
- Category V: Upper Centre

In urban areas the built-up area will be assigned almost area-wide to category I. In rural areas settlement cores are to be identified, which can take on the necessary central functions.

Minimum requirements for basic centres would have to be determined, using the catalogue of facilities of the spatial structure plan of Saxony, for instance (Appendix E.2). This is problematic because, on the one hand, the demands of the affected individuals differ substantially depending on population density and the current equipment. On the other hand, demands seeming to belong to a basic supply – like the existence of shopping facilities for everyday necessities within walking distance – are unlikely to be realised in rural areas under current conditions.

In fact, model projects like "neighbourhood shop" (Bundesministerium für Raumordnung, Bauwesen und Städtebau, 1995; Hessisches Ministerium für Wirtschaft, 1994; Junker, 2006) showed that workable concepts of neighbourhood supply are even possible for sparsely populated areas. However, under pure market economy conditions, the profitability of local shops in rural areas seems difficult to achieve because of the high individual mobility caused by the great degree of motorisation.[67]

These problems can be reduced by differentiating the catalogue of facilities according to regional categories and setting higher standards for urban than for rural areas. A further differentiation is possible between existing and newly-planned settlements. The standards for existing settlements should be formulated moderately, so

[67] Kentmann (1980) determines lower boundaries for the profitability of different facilities. These boundaries vary depending on numerous factors, see Müller, 1999.

that their implementation is actually feasible in present settlement structures. For newly planned settlements, the population density and the transport connection to existing settlement and transport structures can be planned so that the profitability of the facilities is also secured by more ambitious minimum standards.

For any planning, a good neighbourhood supply, based on strict minimum standards, is an important condition for that, on the one hand, all people can satisfy their basic needs and, on the other, all people satisfy these needs with less cost and effort, and with less environmental impact.

Table 3 shows possible configurations of the basic centres. This category would take over a part of the present functions of small centres – with the goal of facilitating an arrangement of these functions as closely to homes as possible. The configuration of centres of higher levels of centrality can be realised according to the spatial structure plan of Saxony. The catalogue for higher level centres includes those facilities of the respective lower levels and/or modifies them.

Category	Existing settlement areas	Areas to be planned newly
Rural area		
I: Basic centre	• General store including: post office counter, access to drugs, cash machine, lottery, dry cleaning and repairs counter, copy service, mail-order business • Weekly surgery (general practitioner and dentist) • Multi-purpose area • "Public area"– e.g. sports field, playground	• General store including: post office counter, access to drugs, cash machine, lottery, dry cleaning and repairs counter, copy service, mail-order business • Weekly surgery (general practitioner and dentist) • Child care up to elementary school • Multi-purpose area • "Public area" – e.g. sports field, playground
Urban area		
I: Basic centre	• Shop (Goods for everyday needs) • Child care up to elementary school • General practitioner and dentist • Playground, green space	• Shop (Goods for everyday needs) • Child care up to elementary school • General practitioner and dentist • Pharmacy • Playground, green space • Restaurant • Financial institute
All categories		
II; III; IV; V	• Facilities according to the spatial structure plan of Saxony (Appendix E.2)	

Table 3: Possible components of a basic transportation supply: spatial planning components – equipment of central places.

C.2.2.2.2 Transport components

The prerequisite for making the central locally distributed facilities actually attainable for the inhabitants is the connection of central places to each other as well as to housing. Here the transport components of the minimum standards are addressed. Suggestions for reference values of these components are found in numerous sources. Reference values for individual motorised transport are given by the German Society for Transport Science (Forschungsgesellschaft für Straßen- und Verkehrswesen (FGSV)) (FGSV, 1988, 1992). Furthermore, data concerning travel times of public transport can be found. These data vary enormously depending on the respective goals of the studies (Gerike, 2005).[68]

When designing the linkage of central places as one component of a basic transportation supply, a focus on public transport is recommended. This is because the

[68] Such target values for public transport are defined in most local public transport plans and regional plans in Germany (Eichmann, 2006).

travel times in individual motorised transport are, in most cases, already very low and bike and foot transport are hardly relevant to the linkage of central places of higher levels of centrality. Moreover, standards for individual motorised transport are only useful for a part of the population and thus, cannot meet the requirement of providing a basic transportation supply for all people.

The linkage of central places to each other and to housing locations can be described by cost items like complex travel times (Schnabel, 1997), which take into consideration travel times, access and leaving times and operating frequencies.[69] Beyond travel times between the centres, the quality of public transport services should be included (density of stops, operating times, amount of seating provided).[70]

To determine these basic transportation supply components, one can rely on local public transport plans, in which standards for operational qualities are listed in detail, distinguished by area categories and operating times.[71]

The system of minimum standards to be developed here should focus on the real minimum demand for operational quality, the area-wide realisation of which seems feasible and meaningful.

The quality of transport links can be operationalised by area-shares or population-shares outside of "public-transport-iso-costs" as lines of equal cost and effort from one reference point.[72] Using population-shares is more advisable than the determination of areas outside the iso-costs, but determining these variables requires considerable data-collecting and computation effort. Using bee-line distances cannot be recommended, since there is only a weak correlation to the travel times of public transport.

A decisive field of a basic transportation supply is the neighbourhood, because most basic needs are satisfied within this space.[73] In this field, minimum standards for foot and bike traffic are vital, since they represent the most favourable alternatives

---

69 These can be considered by average waiting times.

70 Qualitative aspects like the range of products offerd in shops should also be considered for the spatial components of a basic transportation supply, since a comprehensive offer of facilities does not yield any benefit, if it is not used due to a lack of quality.

71 In most cases it is distinguished by peak, secondary and low traffic times (Land Berlin, 2001; Pampel, 1981).

72 In many cases, isochrones are used as lines of equal travel time starting from a certain point, but iso-money and the like are also conceivable.

73 Here, above all, functions that were assigned to the basic centres in chapter C.2.2.2.1, are adressed.

for short distances, both from an ecological and economic viewpoint. In the neighbourhood there is great potential for increasing the modal split portion of the environmentally friendly transport modes: Already 59 percent of all trips are shorter than five kilometres, and in motorised individual transport this share is 43 percent.[74] The portion of short distance trips can be further increased by good accessibility to nearby destinations. Distance measures are conceivable as minimum standards for the neighbourhood, but further criteria like the quality of town layout should be included.

The following possible transport components of a basic transportation supply result:

- Distance measures for foot and bike traffic in the neighbourhood, for instance maximum distance of x meters to a shop (e.g. general store[75]) for y per cent of the population;
- Measures for cost and effort like time, money, comfort or combined measures for linking housing and central places as well as central places to each other;
- Density of stops for public transport, for instance maximum stop distance of x meters for y percent of the population;
- Operating frequency of public transport, for instance frequencies differentiated by different traffic times.

All theses components have to be designed as minimum standards; providing too many offers that are not used leads to wastefulness, damages the environment and increases urban sprawl.[76] Therefore, we must examine thoroughly which transport offers are really necessary for satisfying basic human needs and how such a basic transportation supply can be guaranteed at the lowest possible expenditure.

C.2.3 Participation

Apart from the formulation of transport and spatial planning components discussed in the preceding chapters, the second aspect of a basic transportation supply is the involvement of the affected individuals in its design (established as the basis of the

---

74 See http://www.kontiv2002.de/engl/index.htm, 4.2.2007.

75 See the components of basic centres suggested in chapter C.2.2.2.1.

76 The danger of such oversised offers seems not to be relevant concerning public transport, however, due to money shortages.

social task field in chapter C.2.1). In the literature of transport science, such involvement is described by the term participation (DVWG, 2001; Feindt, 2005; ILS, 2001). This term originates in Latin and means taking part in something, sharing in something, being involved in something. The Enquête commission describes the term as *"voluntary activities from citizens for the purpose of influencing decisions in different levels of the political system."* (Enquête, 2002, p. 125)

The necessity of participation was derived in chapter B.4 from the need-theoretical view. The importance of the involvement of the population is also highlighted in the context of sustainable development. One of the four parts of the final document of the Conference on Environment and Development in 1992 in Rio de Janeiro is dedicated to the empowerment of people: *"One of the fundamental prerequisites for the achievement of sustainable development is broad public participation in decision-making."* (UN, 1992, 23.2.)

In Germany numerous possibilities for the inclusion of people are statutory:[77] It is possible to exert influence on politics by taking part in elections or by joining parties. The referendum is a further option for expressing and possibly implementing opinions. Procedures for the affected individuals to exert an influence on the arrangement of their surrounding are also fixed on a legal basis (Gerhardt, 2007; Holtkamp, 2006; Pound, 2003; Zegras, 2002). Beyond that, there are numerous forms of participation which are not legally anchored.

Consequently, the question is not **whether** people are to participate, since broad consent meets the affirmative answer of this question. The question to be answered within the context of sustainable transportation development is, rather, **how** people are to participate – how a system of sharing could be designed to permit people to articulate and satisfy their needs.

There are various possibilities for meeting this requirement: The levels of participation range from information via perception and consideration to cooperation and joint decision-making (Decker, 2001; DVWG, 2001). All steps of public participation are relevant for the establishment of a basic transportation supply, because purely informing the affected individuals is not sufficient for getting them involved in the

[77] See Dienel, 2002; Enquête, 2002 for the discussion of which of the influencing options should be covered by the term participation.

planning process. The information level is an indispensable prerequisite for the success of any participation and is a component of practically all forms of inclusion.[78] The emphasis of participatory procedures is on the middle levels. Here the most important tasks and possibilities of citizens' participation are found. The last level of real joint decision-making is a very demanding form of inclusion, the implementation of which can mean substantial difficulties, and which requires the power and will for decision-making of all involved parties.

Which procedure for the inclusion of the affected is most suitable depends on the respective problem, the individuals involved and the means available. The range of possible participation procedures is large and ranges from site inspections with the residents via advisory councils, to mediation, to planning cells and citizens' juries.[79] Pros and cons of the procedures must be weighed in every specific case in order to design and implement a case-specific procedure. The selection of suitable procedures and their case-specific adaptation according to the respective circumstances are important success criteria for the implementation of measures. Giving a general and valid recommendation for which participation procedure to choose is not possible due to such differing circumstances.

> The final arrangement of participation procedures in the context of the social task field can be determined only locally for specific applications.

Despite these case-specifics, it is necessary to fix the framework for participation on a superordinate level. If this framework is missing, there might be no or only minor inclusion of the affected in decision-making, due to lack of time or money. That would be undesirable both from the need-theoretical view as well as from view of the sustainable development debate. Thus, the situation concerning participation is similar to the determination of transport and spatial planning components of a basic transportation supply. All these components of the social task field are characterised by the need for normative decisions and by high application specifics.

Therefore, higher-level authorities should concentrate on setting the framework for participation and on limiting it to the fundamental aspects. One vital point covered

---

78 See Gerike, 2005 for an overview of forms of public relations work.

79 See Gerike, 2005 for an overview of important procedures and a suggestion for a method for assessing them; see also Decker, 2001; Dienel, 2002; DVWG, 2001; Enquête, 2002; FGSV, 2002; http://www.buergergutachten.com/en/, 10.1.2007.

by the framework should be the obligation to establish participation procedures as well as their degree of intensity. Figure 13 shows the range of participation intensity and describes variants of the superordinate framework for participation.

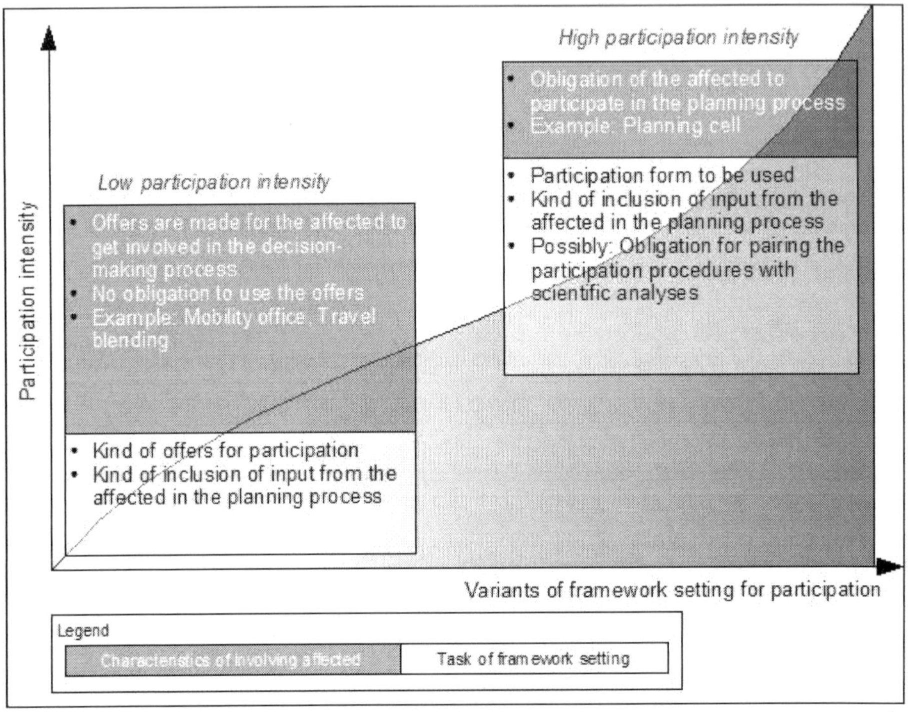

Figure 13: Range of participation intensity regulated by a superordinate framework in the context of establishing a basic transportation supply.

Low participation intensities are characterised by providing the possibility to people to take part in the set-up of a basic transportation supply. The affected individuals can get involved by using the offers of public authorities, but are not obliged to do so. The extent of participation in this variant depends, therefore, on the engagement of local governments in particular, as well as on the affected individuals. The institutional framework set by higher-level authorities only determines what the offers of public authorities look like.

In the case of high participation intensities, the affected individuals are directly addressed by local administrations and are asked to participate in the set-up of a basic transportation supply. With the help of the participative procedures fixed by the superordinate framework, a societal discussion of local transport problems is initiated.

Beyond the participation intensity, the superordinate framework should also govern how the results of realised participation procedures are to flow into the decision-making process.

A further possible component of the framework is the obligation of public planning agencies to accompany the realised participation procedures by scientific analyses. This is based on the assumption that objective deficits concerning the basic transportation supply can be found, deficits that go beyond the knowledge won by cooperation with the affected individuals within participation procedures. The aim is to give recommendations for reducing objective deficits from a scientific viewpoint. These investigations can be done with the help of activity space and accessibility analyses (Axhausen, 2004; Hammer, 2002; Schlich, 2003; Schönfelder, 2003).

The form in which the scientific conclusions flow into the planning process must be decided locally. It seems favourable to use the knowledge as input for the participation procedures in order to develop and evaluate a list of deficits and demands from scientific analysis and from the criticism of the participating individuals. However, it is also conceivable to base the planning exclusively on scientific analysis by referring to its recommendations as fixed components of the basic transportation supply. Here, scientific analysis can only be supplemented by criticism coming out of the participation procedures.

There are numerous possibilities for regulating participation. These lie between the two extremes of high versus low participation intensity shown in Figure 13. The variants differ particularly in the extent of influence of higher-level institutions, in the way they include the affected individuals on site and in the necessary expenditure.

C.2.4 Discussion of criteria for the social task field

In the following chapter, suggestions for criteria for a basic transportation supply are developed based on the insights gained so far. In chapters C.2.4.1 and C.2.4.2, possible components of superordinate minimum standards and of local supplements for spatial planning and transport components are compiled. Moreover, criteria for the process for determining minimum standards and local supplements are necessary. This aspect is discussed in chapter C.2.4.3.

The criterion system to be established for describing the social task field should be absolutely binding in order to guarantee the implementation of the minimum standards and to profit from the above discussed advantages thereof. The discussion of the planning status quo in chapters C.2.2.2.1 and C.2.2.2.2 has shown that the beginnings and recommendations for certain aspects of a basic transportation supply already exist. They can be used as the basis for the following argumentation (Gerike, 2005).

The demand for binding criteria also applies to the superordinate framework within the field of participation: The need-theoretical discussion in chapter B.3 has shown that including the affected individuals in decision-making is indispensable for the establishment of transport development that meets people's needs.

Large problems in current German planning are caused by the lack of mandatory goals: problems related to a lack of financial means as well as to difficulties in the coordination of different plans. Specifically, all planning regulations point to the fact that the concerned municipalities cannot make claims on the implementation of planning targets, since these are only to be fulfilled according to the budget available. Also, neither plans for local public transport nor concepts of transport development for higher planning levels are binding.

C.2.4.1 Minimum standards

In Figure 14 possible components of minimum standards are compiled. The central criterion of spatial planning aspects is the correspondence of the equipment of central places to the facilities indicated in the catalogue of facilities. The following criteria are suitable for the description of transport aspects:

- Proportion of inhabitants outside given distances in the facilities in category I
- Proportion of inhabitants outside of given isolines of public transport (documenting the quality of connection of housing to central places of higher levels, and the quality of connection between central places)

The goal is to meet the minimum standards which must be determined. Success and failure regarding this goal can be documented by using degrees of goal achievement.[80] The question of how to compile and weigh the different possible components of minimum standards is left open here. It is possible to form degrees of goal achievement for every component. These can be displayed separately or compiled to a value of benefit by procedures to be specified.

Therefore, minimum standards describe the fixed part of a basic transportation supply and are suitable for comparing different regions at one time as well as one region at different times.

[80] Which degree of goal achievement stands for achieving the minimum standards must be clarifyed in advance; see Schnabel, 1997, II for possible scales of degrees of goal achievement.

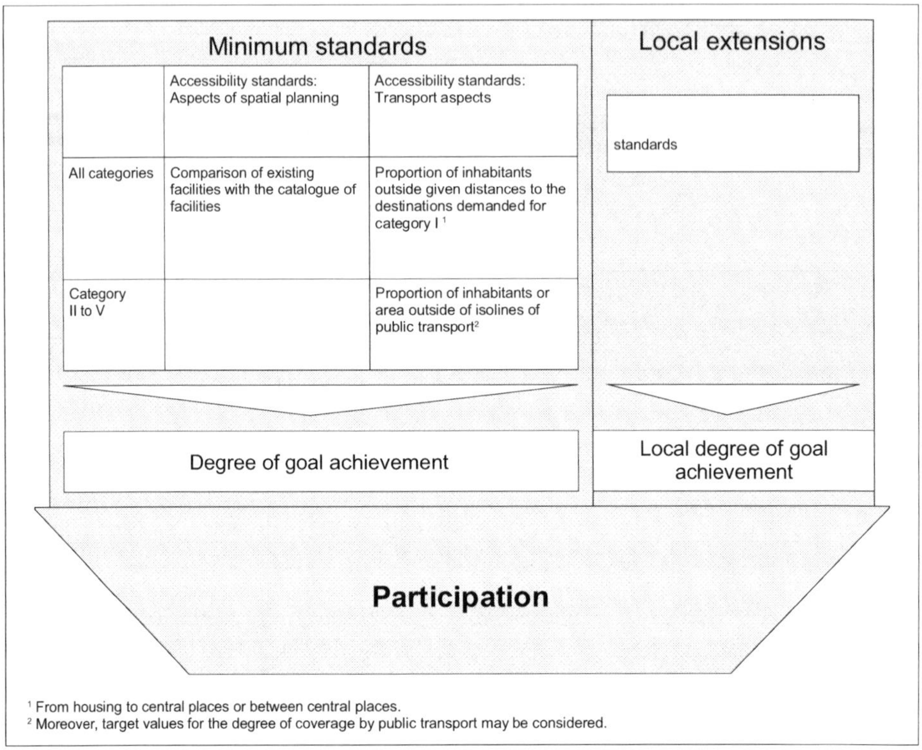

Figure 14: Components of a basic transportation supply, part II: Possible criteria for transport and spatial planning components.

C.2.4.2 Local supplements

Local supplements are goals of a basic transportation supply going beyond the superordinate minimum standards. These goals can be operationalised by the same indicators as minimum standards. Municipalities should have more or less freedom in this field depending on which guidelines for the design of local supplements are given within the superordinate framework of a basic transportation supply:

- If concrete indicators are given by the superordinate framework, then only the target criteria can be varied by the municipalities.
- If no specifications are made by the superordinate framework, then the local supplements can be arranged freely by the municipalities. Depending on the political and financial situation in the municipalities, minimum standards can be extended in all fields or emphasis can be placed on specific fields. It is also possible to formulate access or transport indicators.

Between these two extremes there are various possibilities for restricting the options of the municipalities in the field of a basic transportation supply by superordinate regulations.

For the different components of local supplements, “local” degrees of goal achievement can be formed and possibly compiled to a value of benefit. These options are illustrated in Figure 14. The value of benefit gives an objective picture of to what extent the specific local goals, going beyond the minimum standards, are achieved. However, it is only conditionally suitable for inter-community comparisons. This is because the goals set by specific municipalities (which may serve as yardstick for forming local degrees of goal achievement) probably differ and should differ significantly between the municipalities.

Consequently, local degrees of goal achievement are characterised by their case-specifics. The determination of local supplementary indicators is only possible for concrete applications together with the affected individuals. Here, different stakeholders can participate, including economic stakeholders, in order to negotiate the final set-up of the social task field. The concepts resulting from such discussions may be and should be completely different between the municipalities. It is especially important to consider the problems of people who have only few possibilities for representing and implementing their interests.

C.2.4.3 The process of designing a basic transportation supply

In the following chapter, the focus is less on the criteria of a basic transportation supply and more on the process for determining these criteria. Both minimum standards and local supplements must first be determined and then examined and updated afterwards at regular intervals. The following questions should be raised:

- Do the current minimum standards successfully characterise the transport offers necessary for the satisfaction of basic needs of people?
- Do the local supplements correspond to the basic needs of the locally affected individuals going beyond the minimum standards?
- Are the affected individuals comfortable with the kind and intensity of their inclusion in the organisation of the basic transportation supply?

To answer these questions accessibility analyses can be carried out, the results of which can be contrasted with values recommended according to current scientific knowledge, or with activity space analyses as a measure of the efficiency of the offers. Beyond that, surveys should be conducted in order to convey the general atmosphere:[81] Is the topic of sustainable transportation development well-known? Are the offers of public authorities for participation well-known to the affected individuals? Do they agree with the offers for participation? What are the most important components of a basic transportation supply from view of the affected individuals?

In Figure 15 possible criteria and procedures for the process of determining a basic transportation supply are shown in the middle text box, since they are relevant to minimum standards, local supplements and questions of participation.

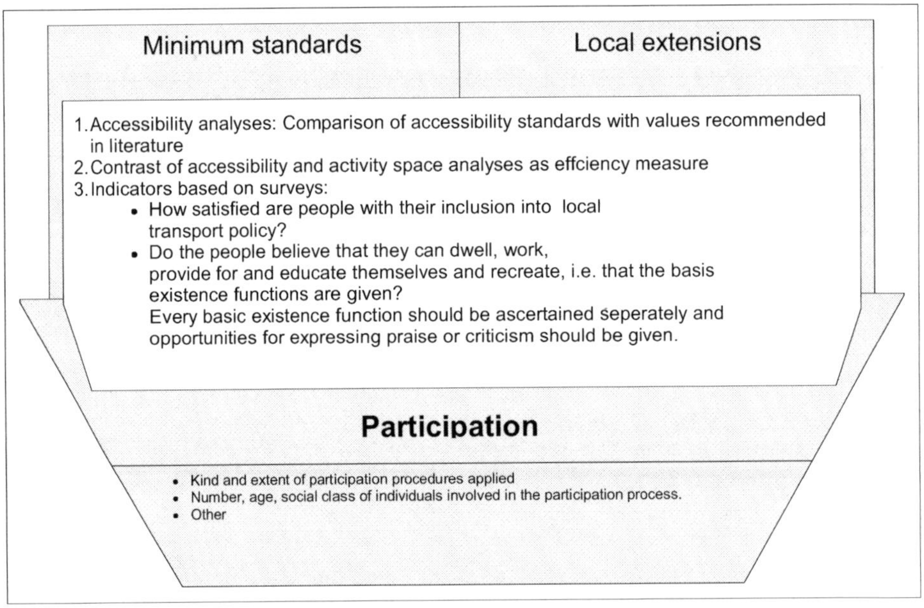

Figure 15: Components of a basic transportation supply, part III: Possible analysis criteria for the process of determining and modifying transport and spatial planning components.

The field of participation should be similarly regulated to transport and spatial planning components by a superordinate framework setting. The recommendation for using high participation intensities and a binding framework was derived from the need-theoretical discussion. The following criteria of a superordinate framework setting, listed in the lower part of Figure 15, are conceivable:

81 See Gerike, 2005 for an overview of surveys in the transport sector.

- Kind and extent of participation procedures applied
- Number, age and socio-economic status of individuals involved in the participation process

As with transport and spatial minimum standards, the superordinate framework in the field of participation can be extended on a local level in order to involve the affected individuals more intensively in the organisation of the basic transportation supply.

C.3 The resource task field

The subject of the resource task field, as was established in chapter B.4.2.2.4, is the intra- and intergenerational distribution of natural resources.

To concretise this task field, an initial overview of possible categorisations of the term of natural resources is given in chapter C.3.1. Goals for the consumption of natural resources, discussed in literature, are presented in chapter C.3.2. Finally, in chapter C.3.3, possible criteria for the resource task field in the context of sustainable transportation development are derived.

C.3.1 The term “natural resources”

All natural resources used by humans, such as raw material or land, can be included in the formulation of limits for the consumption of natural resources by the transport sector within the resource task field. These examples concern the cause-side of environmental impacts.[82] In terms of the impact-side, limits for the maximum cost to ecosystems can be set. Examples thereof are decreasing biodiversity, climate change and the depletion of the ozone layer.

Siebert (1983, p. 2) defines natural resources as *“goods, provided by nature for fulfilling human desires directly or indirectly”* and thereby focuses mainly on the formation-side. Figure 16 shows a possible structuring of the term natural resources. Initially,

[82] Depending on the interpretation of the term resource, the resource “human being” can also be included. As with other natural resources, it is also “damaged” and therefore “used,” so that the formulation of limits seems to be justified also for those impacts of transport that only affect humans.

natural resources can be divided by their means of production in nature, by their intended use and by the possibility of applying the exclusion principle.[83]

Renewable and non-renewable resources are then distinguished within the means of production in nature.[84] Renewable resources originate in biological growth processes. Non-renewable resources include all resources for which natural developing processes, like sedimentation, are not relevant to human planning horizons.

With regard to excludability, resources are divided into private and public goods.[85] The earth's atmosphere and the oceans, for instance, can be counted among the latter. Furthermore, natural resources can be divided according to their use in consumer goods and production factors.

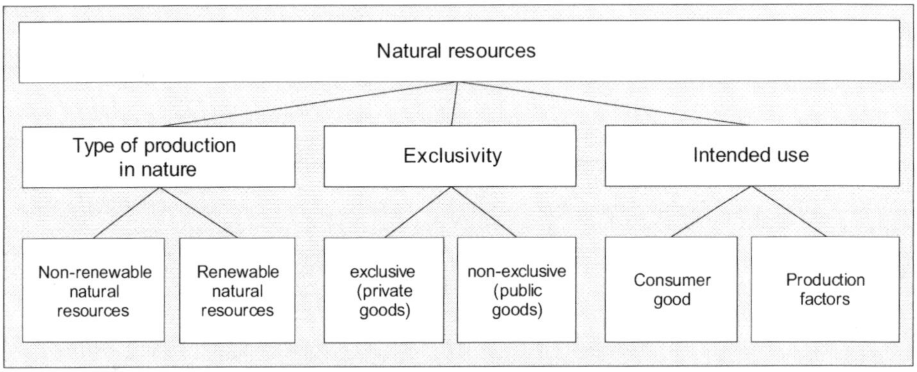

Figure 16: Natural resources, according to Siebert (1983).

The MIPS concept covers the following input categories for the systematisation of material-inputs:[86]

- Abiotic raw materials: minerals, fossil energy carriers, unused extraction, soil excavation
- Biotic raw materials: Plant biomass from cultivation, plant biomass not from cultivation, animal biomass not from cultivation

---

83 Further categorisations of natural resources are possible, e.g. according to whether used resources can be re-used (e.g. recovering of ore) or not (e.g. agrarian products).

84 This classification is used by Endres, 1993.

85 Besides the non-excludability, the non-rivalry in consumption is a further criterion of public goods, see chapter C.1.

86 MIPS = Material Service per Service Unit; see Ritthoff, 2002 and http://www.wupperinst.org/Projekte/mipsonline/english.html, 12.6.2006; Here almost all natural resources are addressed. These are to be put in the category of production factors according to Siebert's (1983) subdivision by intended use.

- Earth removal in agriculture and forestry: Active (e.g. ploughed earth), passive (e.g. erosion)
- Water: Process or cooling water, each divided into surface extraction; groundwater extraction; deep groundwater extraction
- Air: Combustion, chemical conversion, physical conversion (aggregate state), other extracted air

The division into these five categories is the result of scientific research and long-term application of the MIPS concept. It is practiced fairly uniformly, so that national and international statistics increasingly use these categories when accounting for material flows. The categorisation is based on the classical division between earth, water and air. The category of earth is subdivided into three individual categories in order to achieve a better expressiveness: abiotic raw materials, biotic raw materials and earth removal.

C.3.2 Goals for the protection of natural resources

Limits for resource consumption in general, and for the transport sector in particular are formulated especially in the context of research on sustainability indicators (Heiland, 2003).

The project Environmentally Sustainable Transport (EST), initiated by the OECD, is especially relevant for the transport sector.[87] In the context of this project, concrete indicators for the transport sector were developed, regarding the impact side in particular. Table 4 gives an overview of the formulated reduction goals. The environmental impacts considered are examples of the fact that in the transport sector impact chains with several links often exist. All items are simultaneously environmental impacts of transport and causes of secondary environmental problems, except in case of the land consumption as an explicitly cause-sided criterion. For instance NO_x and VOC are responsible for the formation of noxious ozone and are involved in the over-fertilisation and acidification of soil and water. Particles (PM) and noise damage human health.

[87] See SRU, 2005 for goals of environmental protection in the transport sector for Germany.

Parameter	Criterion		Specification
CO_2	-80%	Emission reduction in the transport sector in 2030 compared to 1990	All areas
NO_x	-90%		
VOC	-90%		
PM	-99%		Urban areas
Noise	<= 65 dB(A)		All areas
	<= 55 dB(A) daytime		Residential areas
	<= 45 dB(A) nighttime		
Land consumption	Criterion still needs to be developed		Urban areas
	No new road building for main roads		Rural areas

Table 4: EST-criteria for the German case study, according to Verron, 2001.

C.3.3 Discussion of criteria for the resource task field

The questions to be treated within the resource task field are diverse and closely intertwined. This complexity can be handled by using key-criteria, the variation of which can support sustainability in as many fields as possible.

The CO_2-emissions represent such a key criterion concerning the environmental effects of transport. They are directly related to energy use and therefore to the use of limited natural resources. Furthermore, CO_2 is an important greenhouse gas, and the reduction of CO_2-emissions is thus an important goal of climate protection. The need to lower CO_2-emissions is increasingly accepted and is the subject of international negotiations at different levels. Furthermore, the problems in this area are serious and urgent: Climate processes are long-term and inertial mechanisms, so that early action is vital in order to avoid undesired developments.

> For these reasons the CO_2-emissions of transport are recommended as key criteria for the resource task field.

However, for a comprehensive analysis criteria should also be developed for the other variables discussed in chapter C.3.1 in order to identify problems and appropriately design measures.

C.4 Recommendations for designing sustainable transportation development

C.4.1 General conclusions

It becomes obvious from the task fields compiled that the focus of activities in transport planning for implementing sustainable transportation development should be on the social task field in particular. In this context, particular measures for directly influencing accessibility by changing spatial structures and/or transport offers are addressed using the term transport planning.

The job of the resource task field is to set limits for the consumption of natural resources, limits which must be met by the other task fields. In the allocative task field, the framework is set for market transactions with the aim of developing the qualities of the market mechanism to articulate and satisfy human needs as freely as possible. Thus, the allocative and the resource task field set the legal and financial framework. Within this framework, people can choose their transport behaviour freely – according to their individual preferences. However, the job of the social task field is the direct modification of spatial resistances by changing spatial planning and transport structures.

Therefore, an important result of this work is the realisation that transport planning in its design task (by directly influencing accessibility) can concentrate largely on the guarantee of a basic transportation supply. The task is not to satisfy all the mobility needs that are expressed by increasing distances, for instance. The focus should instead be on the satisfaction of basic needs, which is to be guaranteed for all people.

The satisfaction of needs, going beyond such a basic transportation supply, is to be dealt with the allocative task field, because the market was established as the most flexible mechanism for the articulation and satisfaction of needs. The interaction of offer and demand reaches balances which enable the efficient satisfaction of human needs in the case of functioning market mechanisms.

In order to achieve a basic transportation supply, a societal discussion about how this supply should look is first necessary. Options for answering this question were discussed in chapter C.2. The final definition of such a basic transportation supply requires political decisions: What kind of mobility can and should be guaranteed for all people? Measures for the implementation of the formulated goals only become possible and necessary by answering this question. These measures do not react to observed or predicted developments, but influence the transport system consciously, with regard to the determined goals.

This focus of planning measures on the social task field corresponds to the view of a modern state as was formulated in the government programme "Modern State – Modern Administration" of the Federal Government of Germany in 1999. This government programme is based on the principle of the enabling state: Citizens should do on their own what they can do as well as or better than the state, not only to disburden the state, but also because a state that takes over all activities is paralysing to society. Citizens' engagement can unfold with difficulty if the state declares itself responsible for everything (Enquête, 2002; Federal Ministry of the Interior, 2004). Therefore, the task of the state is to restrict its activities to the fields in which too much is expected from the individual.

The distribution of natural resources to be formulated within the resource task field has to be binding in order to guarantee its target limits. These should be exclusion criteria for measures in the social task field; if the planned measures exceed the limits given by the resource task field, they must not be realised.

Formulating exclusion criteria is also possible in the other task fields. In the social task field the failure to comply with the superordinate minimum standards as a lower limit of the development corridor can be formulated as an exclusion criterion. In the case of financial restrictions, measures may be only implemented if they do not exceed the available budget. Target values for external costs are also suitable as exclusion criterion.

The points discussed result in a conceivable course of transport planning oriented to the goal of sustainable transportation development, which is shown in Figure 17. The starting point and central goal of such planning should be to guarantee a basic transportation supply within the framework of the social task field. This basic supply has to be operationalised within the phase of pre-orientation and problem analysis by defining concrete criteria for individual cases of application. This should be done within a broad societal discussion. The components of the basic supply may and will differ between municipalities and application cases. This is caused by the variability of human needs and is therefore desirable. However, it is important to fix the individual targets in advance in order to have definite target criteria for planning.

In the investigation of measures phase, measures are selected for the implementation of the determined basic transportation supply. They are then evaluated regarding the goal of sustainable transportation development. Impacts of measures are modelled and unsuitable measures are eliminated based on the exclusion criteria determined in the preceding phases of planning. The remaining measures can be evaluated by formalised assessment procedures. Based on the assessment results, decisions can be made and the selected measures can be implemented.

An important point is regular impact control of realised measures as a prerequisite for the revision and, if necessary, the modification of input and the framework of transport planning. Through this feedback the planning cycle starts again. The aim should be to update the planning regularly in order to meet the process character of sustainable transportation development.

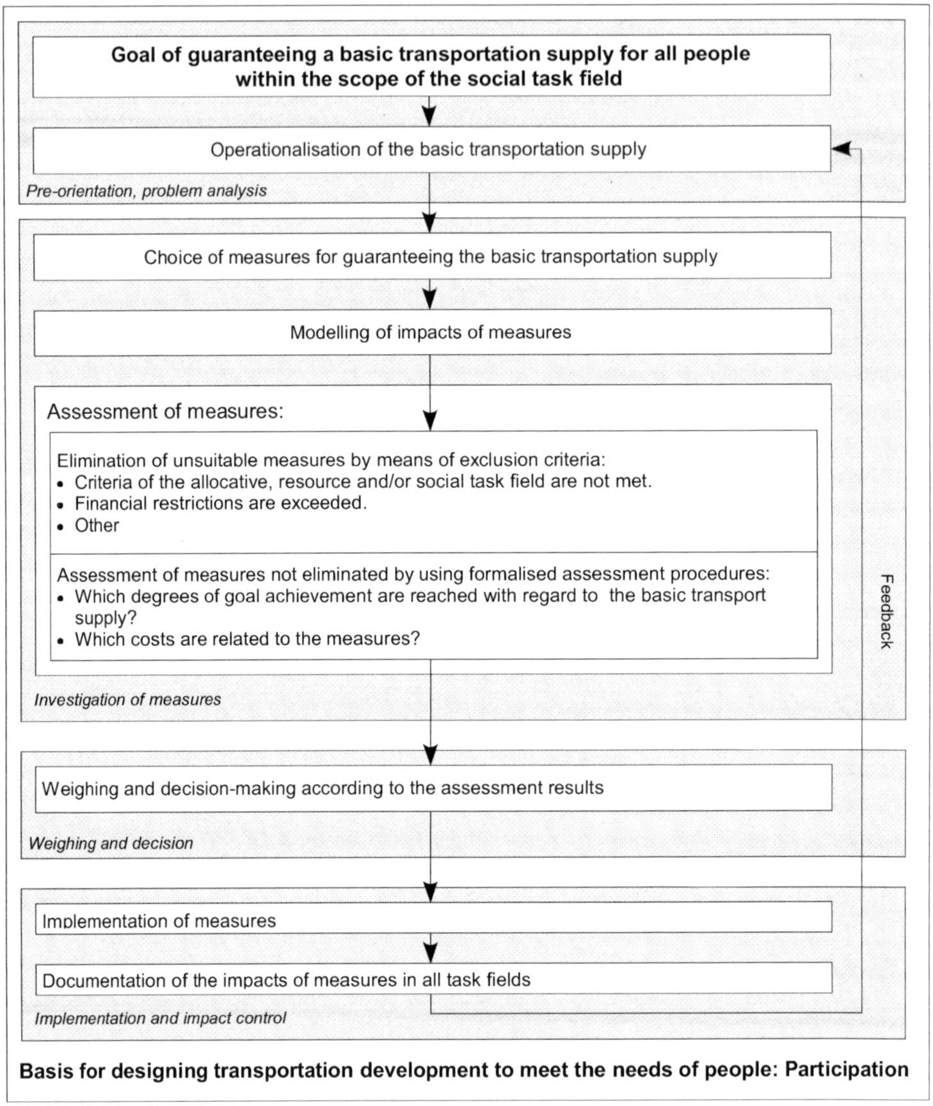

Figure 17: Conceivable course of transport planning oriented to the goal of sustainable transportation development.

C.4.2 Steps for implementation

A first important step for the realisation of sustainable transportation development is the final operationalisation of the three task fields. The level of administration responsible for this should be set as high as possible in order to ensure an area-wide scope of the criteria. German federal or European institutions seem suitable for this. An exception is local supplements as components of the basic transportation supply to be determined within the social task field. These can be set case-specifically on the municipal level or partly on the regional or federal state level (nationwide).

Questions to be discussed within the allocative and resource task field are already in the realm of these administrative levels. Pricing measures for internalisation can be planned and implemented mainly on the European and federal level. Options for reducing CO_2-emissions are discussed and negotiated worldwide. Currently, the federal states in Germany, in particular, as well as subordinated institutions are responsible for the definition of criteria falling in the social task field. This distribution of competences can be maintained for the design of local supplements. However, minimum standards as the foundation of the basic transportation supply should be determined at least on the federal level. Table 5 summarises the suggested distribution of responsibilities.

Task field	Task	Possible responsible level of administration
Social task field	Determination of transport and spatial planning minimum standards	Federal level
	Framework-setting for participation	Federal level
	Determination of local extensions	Municipality, federal state
Allocative task field	Determination of indicators and target values	Federal level
Resource task field	Determination of indicators and target values	Federal level

Table 5: Responsibilities for the final determination of the task fields for sustainable transportation development.

Following the final determination of the task fields, steps for implementation can be taken. Orientation to existing planning structures is recommended for choosing institutions on which to place the responsibility for the implementation of federal level criteria. In the social task field, the guarantee of the minimum standards is the first task for the respective planning authorities before the components of a basic transportation supply going beyond the minimum standards can be fixed and realised.

In the implementation many fields of policy must be integrated. This results from the complexity of the problems to be treated: Transport touches all fields of our lives, and measures of almost all political fields have impacts on transport.[88] The circle of relevant stakeholders can be extended beyond the political realm because the cooperation of media, local enterprises and so on is also necessary for implementing the goal of sustainable transportation development.

Therefore, the networking of planning and decision-making institutions is an important prerequisite for the realisation of a transport system meeting the needs of people.[89] The currently practiced stepped planning in Germany combined with the feedback principle provides good opportunities for this networking, since it enables planning and decision-making authorities to decide the questions they are concerned with at their individual planning level.[90]

An important point to be considered for the implementation of sustainable transportation is the interdependency between the task fields. It is necessary, for instance, to develop criteria for deciding between different alternatives to meet the limits given by the resource task field. Here, orientation to the aims of the basic transportation supply is recommended. Measures in the allocative task field can also support meeting the set limits.

The municipal level is of special importance for designing a need-oriented transport development. On this level the basic transportation supply is finally determined by developing specific local supplements. Today's transport planning on this level is characterised by great differences concerning both the extent of planning and the distribution of competences. Furthermore, local transport planning is affected to a

88 A method for examining transport impacts of measures of non-transport policy fields is the check of strategic conformity in Zürich (Tiefbauamt der Stadt Zürich, 2002).

89 This concept is called integrative transport planning (Holz-Rau, 2002).

90 See Turowski, 2002 for an explanation of the feedback principle.

large extent by implementation problems stemming from financial shortages and the influences of superordinate planning levels. For numerous municipalities, there are transport concepts, which are ambitious but rarely implemented (Koch, 2001). These problems can be remedied by institutionalising the municipal transport planning in close relation to urban planning.[91]

C.4.3 Increasing acceptance

Measures that have low acceptance rates are not implemented or their implementation is related to serious difficulties. The heuristic acceptance model of Schlag shows that the acceptance of measures increases when social pressure to accept the measures is perceived, when personal advantages are expected from the measure and when the measure is regarded as effective (Schade, 2000, 2003a, 2003b, Schlag, 2000; Widmer, 2000).

This knowledge can be used to increase the chances of implementing measures for supporting sustainable transportation development successfully:

- By pointing out the benefit of measures: People's options for carrying out activities to satisfy their needs will be extended and not restricted by these measures, especially in neighbourhood.
- On a similar note, the effectiveness of orientation to a basic transportation supply can be communicated. Compact settlement structures, which are aimed at in order to realise good nearby supply, incur significantly fewer costs than dispersed structures – for the individual transport user as well as for public budgets.
- The social pressure can be increased by including opinion leaders into the realisation of measures.

[91] See Koch, 2001 for a suggestion for a municipal transport planning law. It provides a good starting point for organising sustainable transport planning on the local level. An important point is the bindingness of planning in order to secure implementation.

C.5 Consequences for the assessment of measures

The topic of the present work is to concretise the goal of sustainable transportation development, and thus the transport planning phase of establishing objectives (FGSV, 2000; Litman, 2006c). This phase is an important prerequisite for the further course of planning, since within it criteria are determined for analysing the status quo and identifying deficiencies. The analysis of the status quo forms the basis for the development of concepts for action in the phases of investigation and assessment of measures.

In the following chapter, the consequences of the insights gained for the subsequent planning phases so far are discussed. The goals discussed for the task fields in the preceding chapters can for the most part be achieved by different means. How to decide then, which method is best? Which of the numerous available measures should be chosen? The following chapter is dedicated answering to these questions.

C.5.1 Introduction

Decisions in the transport sector are characterised by high complexity: The transport system is connected to numerous sectors of society and the environment, meaning that measures implemented in the transport sector have impacts on almost all sectors of society and vice versa. Assessment procedures were developed to reduce this complexity and to rationalise and standardise decision-making. Assessment procedures serve to develop value judgements concerning complex issues in order to prepare political decisions (Schnabel, 1997: II).

To make this complex reality assessable, models with different degrees of elaboration are used in assessment procedures. The more detail a model uses to describe reality, the more complex and difficult it is to handle. Simple models represent reality in less detail.

Furthermore, assessment procedures always contain normative components, because a weighing of different positive and negative impacts is necessary in almost all cases. Are higher speeds in motorised individual transport enabled by extending a road more important than damages to the health of residents due to increased noise levels, for example? Win-win situations can rarely be realised.

Decision makers must still answer these questions, even if they use assessment procedures. These are auxiliary instruments that are necessary to reveal the criteria of assessment, to standardise the methodology of assessment and to make different cases comparable. However, it is important to use the procedures cautiously and to know the methods and assumptions behind them. Only then can assessment procedures develop their advantages.

The following remarks are consciously restricted to sketch possible rough structures of assessment procedures, because a detailed devolvement of such assessment methods would far exceed the scope of the present work. The main task of the following chapter is to indicate the consequences for the assessment of measures, resulting from the goal of need-oriented transport development, as previously defined. Options for considering this goal in assessment procedures are sketched.

C.5.2 Conclusions for designing assessment procedures regarding the goal of sustainable transportation development

Before the decision for certain assessment methods can be made, we must answer the question of whether to include only impacts that that can be monetised, or whether also to consider impacts that can not be monetised. This problem in particular is under debate for the benefits of transport measures, since most of the cost components are available in monetary units or can be transformed into monetary units. Two points become apparent when analysing the currently applied assessment procedures for measures in the transport sector, with regard to the benefit components considered (Gerike, 2005; Schnabel, 1997):

- The benefit components flowing into assessment often describe cost and effort by interpreting their reductions as benefits.
- In many cases, benefits that can be monetised, are quantified exclusively.

This approach, however, seems unsatisfying, with regard to the insights gained in the present work. On the one hand, the clear separation of costs and benefits is necessary and, on the other hand, so is the consideration of all benefit components, including the ones that cannot be monetised. Which "true" benefits are to be included in the assessment of measures for supporting sustainable transportation development? As a result of the discussion in the preceding chapters, the benefit of measures means that, in contrast to the "do-nothing-case," people are able, or are better able, to carry out the activities necessary to satisfy their needs.

Such changes are covered mainly by the criteria of the social task field. However, the criteria of the allocative and resource task fields represent costs that should include internal and external components. Measures are more favourable, the lower these costs are.

Consequently, the stated benefits are found mainly in the basic transportation supply, which has to be guaranteed within the social task field. Activities necessary for satisfying human needs can be better realised if spatial resistances decrease – either by shorter distances or by better possibilities for overcoming unchanged distances.

An important prerequisite for using the basic transportation supply for the assessment of measures is the quantitative determination of this term. Besides superordinate minimum standards, the basic transportation supply will differ significantly from municipality to municipality. This is desirable because of the individual needs in the different municipalities, if the local supplements of minimum standards are bindingly defined.

In this case, the aim of the planned measures is to achieve the determined basic transportation supply at minimal expenditure. Here, the minimum principle is addressed as part of the term efficiency. A resource use can be called efficient if a determined goal is achieved at minimum costs. In contrast, the maximum principle aims at achieving a maximum benefit through a fixed input (Blum, 2000).

The following conclusions result for operationalising the benefits of measures by using the criteria of a basic transportation supply:

- If the criteria of a basic transportation supply are not fulfilled, the benefits to be assessed lie mainly in approaching the aim of a basic transportation supply. It does not seem possible to monetise such benefits, but the use of degrees of goal achievement, as used in the value benefit analysis, is conceivable.[92] In this case, the goal would be to fulfil all determined criteria of the basic transportation supply.[93]
- If the basic transportation supply is already reached, there are two possibilities:
    - New supplementary goals can be formulated on the municipal level and then used as yardstick for assessment.
    - Alternatively, a benefit indicator can be developed to allow for indicating the benefits realised by the measures. The development of such an indicator presents substantial difficulties, because transport is a complex, highly interrelated system. Eventually, the description of the benefits can be realised by using accessibility indicators or the inclusion of approaches of welfare theory (Tavasszy, 2004).

On the cost side, assessment is easier: All internal and external costs incurred by the measures have to be assessed as expenditures. These are available to a large degree in monetary units or can be transformed into monetary units. Only the monetising of very long-term impacts (like climate change) and of impacts related to land consumption by transport (like separation effects, sealing) is difficult (Quinet, 2004).

The following possibilities for choosing a procedure for assessing measures (for the goal of sustainable transportation development) result from the above discussed points:

[92] See Gerike, 2005; Schnabel, 1997 for a discussion of the value benefit analysis. The transformation of results into degrees of goal achievement is carried out by using functions of degrees of goal achievement (Schnabel, 1997).

[93] See Schnabel, 1997 for the scaling of degrees of goal achievement.

- Cost-benefit-analyses are out of question due to the previously discussed assumption that the benefit components cannot be monetised.[94]
- If cost and effort that can be monetised are considered exclusively, then the application of cost-effectivity analyses[95] is recommended. The quotient from benefits as value of benefit and costs may serve as a decision criterion. This quotient quantifies which benefits can be reached per unit of means employed.
- If cost and effort that can not be monetised should be included, either the value-benefit analysis or a multicriteria analysis is suitable for the assessment of measures (Borken, 2005).[96]

Options for fitting such assessment procedure into the course of transport planning around the goal of sustainable transportation development were discussed in chapter C.4.

94 See Gerike, 2005; Hanusch, 1994; Schnabel, 1997 for a discussion of cost-benefit analysis.

95 See Gerike, 2005; Schnabel, 1997 for a discussion of cost-effectivity analysis.

96 If evidence of efficient input use has to be provided for legal reasons, this can be realised following the assessment by carrying out a supplementary cost-benefit analysis.

D Summary

D.1 Approach

The starting point for the present work is the goal of sustainable transportation development. The prerequisite for implementing this qualitative guideline is its operationalisation – a task which proves difficult due to the process character of sustainable development. However, applying concrete indicators to his term is necessary in order to be able to assess the status quo and realised measures for this goal.

The present work deals with this contradiction between the process character of sustainability and the demand for exact criteria by answering the following questions:

- How can the concept of sustainable transportation development be concretised while simultaneously taking the process character of this concept into consideration?
- Which recommendations for the implementation of measures to encourage sustainable development can be derived?

To address these questions, the term "sustainable development" was initially delineated for the present work. As a result of this working step, the term "needs" was placed at the centre of the work. Sustainable development is regarded as development oriented to the needs of people. Therefore, the first central question to be answered can be modified as follows: How can transport development which aims at meeting human needs be concretised?

The following task fields were established based on the subsequent need-theoretical discussion:

- Allocative task field: The market is a suitable instrument for identifying and satisfying needs. The aim of this task field is therefore to reduce market distortions to allow the qualities of the market mechanism to unfold freely.
- Social task field: Distributive task fields of sustainable transportation are required as a result of the insufficient consideration of distributive aspects by the market mechanism. Social aspects are covered by the first distributive task field known as the social task field. The basis of sustainable transportation develop-

ment is the provision of a basic transportation supply offered by public authorities which has to guarantee the fulfilment of basic needs. It is described by minimum standards and completed by specific local planning. Therefore, the aim of this task field is the guarantee of a basic transportation supply.

- Resource task field: The object of the second distributive task field, the resource task field, is to manage the distribution of natural resources among generations and regions as the precondition for the process of providing transport services.

The three task fields developed were joined into a development corridor:

- The lower boundary is composed of the basic transportation supply to be guaranteed within the social task field. This basic transportation supply should not be fallen short of.
- The upper limit of the corridor, which should not be exceeded, is composed of carrying capacity limits to be formulated within the resource task field.
- The guidelines for all activities within the corridor are to be defined by the allocative task field, the aim of which is to provide functioning market mechanisms.
- Next, options for putting the development corridor into concrete terms were identified. If some of the suggested options are chosen within a societal discussion, the concept of sustainable transportation can be precisely described for concrete application.

Figure 18 summarises the described steps of work:

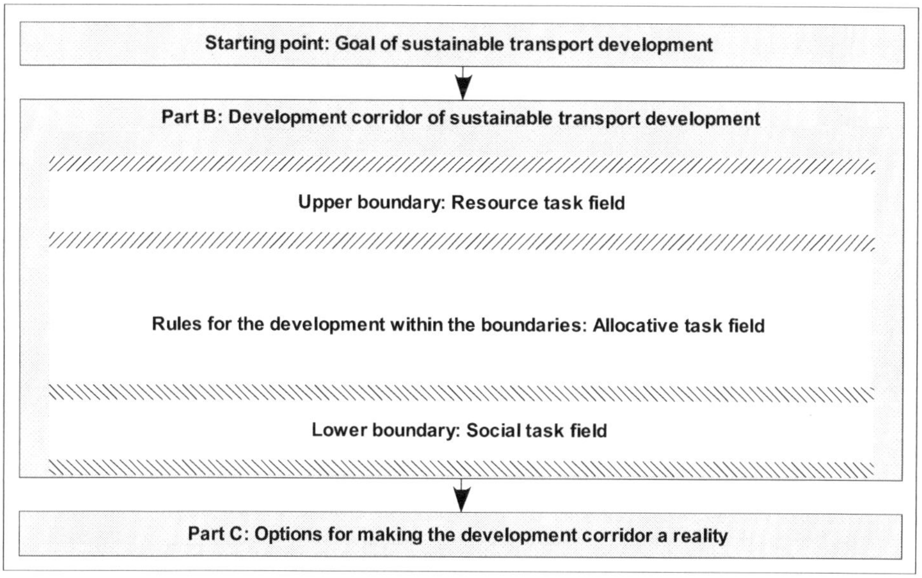

Figure 18: Overview of the steps of the study – Summary.

D.2 Results and recommendations

Based on the insights gained, the following recommendations for measures can be derived:

The real design tasks (as direct changes of spatial resistances) for supporting sustainable transportation development lie firstly in the social task field of guaranteeing a basic transportation supply for all people. The success of measures should not be quantified by the continuous reduction of spatial resistances. Rather, the central criterion should be whether people (or goods for people) can reach the destinations they have to reach in order to satisfy their basic needs. Therefore, transport planning should not react to current and predicted developments like growing transport volumes or increasing distances, but should instead influence the transport system proactively – by concentrating on guaranteeing a basic transportation supply for all people.

The basic transportation supply to be realised within the social task field must be defined with the help of a societal discussion. This discussion is of immense importance for the design of need-oriented transport development. Therefore the following questions must be answered: What kind of transport does society desire and what kind of transport can it afford? Which basic transportation supply should be guaranteed exactly? Initial answers to this question were established.

A second essential design task lies in the satisfaction of all needs beyond the basic ones, preferably by market mechanisms, because these are suitable for the articulation and satisfaction of human needs. The goal of measures within the allocative task field addressed here is to support the unhindered unfolding of the market mechanism qualities. Here, the reduction of external costs is a key criterion; without progress in this field, there is hardly anything to accomplish in the other task fields.

The third essential design task lies in providing limits for the use of natural resources. These must not be exceeded by any activities within the transport sector. The resource task field addressed here has to be determined according to the current state of knowledge and within the scope of a societal discussion.

Therefore, the allocative and resource task fields set the legal and financial framework in which people can choose their transport behaviour according to their individual preferences. However, the objective of the social task field is to directly guarantee people's mobility. This can be done by changing spatial resistances through technical solutions for substituting transport or by changing qualitative items, and so on.

The basis for establishing sustainable transportation development is the inclusion of affected individuals. Science can accompany the participation processes by developing and permanently updating recommendations for designing a basic transportation supply as well as for the internalisation of external costs and for the type and height of limits in the resource task field.

The inclusion of affected individuals was discussed specifically within the social task field. However, people's participation is also essential in the other task fields. Here, especially, aspects of acceptance are important.

The need for research is especially present in the social task field:

- Which offers should be components of a basic transportation supply from the economic standpoint, from private stakeholders' viewpoint and in the eyes of politics? Are there "benefit-maximising" chances for access?
- How do the offers conceived within the basic transportation supply influence transport behaviour?
- How can a good use of the offers be achieved? How can the reactions of people to different transport offers be assessed?

D.3 Final Conclusions

The following conclusions can be drawn regarding the initially posed questions:

- The goal of sustainable transportation development can be concretised without contradicting its process character.
- Here, the task of politics is to determine the development corridor. Staying within the corridor guarantees that the realised measures support sustainable transportation development.
- Within the corridor there is space for the free formation of offer and demand. Such openness for activities and negotiations is necessary, since an ultimate determination of the term "needs" would contradict the variability and inconsistency of this term.

The following requirements were established for the development corridor to limit the space for individual activities:

- Spatial and transport systems must facilitate the satisfaction of basic needs for all people. This need is covered by the social task field. The basic transportation supply to be guaranteed within this task field must not be fallen short of, and it therefore forms the lower boundary of the development corridor.
- The natural resources necessary for providing the transport services must not exceed carrying capacities to be determined. These carrying capacities to be specified within the resource task field form the upper boundary of the corridor.

The most important criterion for all measures within the development corridor is true costs: Only by imposing all costs on the causer, including external components, are the right incentives for human behaviour set, thus facilitating the unfolding of market mechanism qualities for articulating and satisfying human needs.

Finally, the process character of sustainability could be confirmed in all steps of this work. The satisfaction of human needs, and thus the goal of sustainable transportation development, must be regarded as a process. Without trying to force an ideal world, this goal must be realised by ever newer individual and societal attempts. We have to be aware of and use the high degree of personal freedom and the readily available resources at our disposal. Together they form a strong basis for implementing sustainable transportation development.

E Appendices

E.1 References

Acker-Widmaier, G. (1999). *Intertemporale Gerechtigkeit und nachhaltiges Wirtschaften - Zur normativen Begründung eines Leitbildes.* Marburg.

Academy for Spatial Research and Planning (ARL) (2005). *Handwörterbuch der Raumordnung.* Hannover.

Albrecht, R. (1977). *Verkehrsbedingungen von benachteiligten Bevölkerungsgruppen als Leitgröße für eine zielorientierte Stadt- und Verkehrsplanung.* On behalf of Ministry of transport, task group for regional planning. Berlin.

Federal Office for Spatial Development (ARE) (2006). *Costs and benefits of transport.* http://www.are.admin.ch/themen/verkehr/00252/00472/00486/index.html?lang=en.

Axhausen, K.W. (2007). Definition of movement and activity for transport modelling. In Hensher, D.A., Button, K.J. (Eds.), *Handbook of Transport Modelling.* (2nd ed.) Oxford: Elsevier, Arbeitsberichte IVT ETH Zürich, 412, http://www.ivt.ethz.ch/vpl/publications/reports.

Axhausen, K.W., Schönfelder, S. (2004). *Measuring the spatial reach of persons, cities or organisations.* STELLA Group 3 meeting. Arlington. January 2004. http://www.ivt.baug.ethz.ch/vrp/vortraege_d.html.

Banister, D. (1994). *Viewpoint: reducing the need to travel through planning.* In: TPR 65 (4) 1994, pp. 349-354.

Bahlburg, M., Kunze, R. (1979). *Orientierungswerte für die Infrastrukturplanung – Analysewerte und Zielindikatoren der Planung in Bund, Ländern und Gemeinden.* Papers of the Academy for Spatial Research and Planning Vol. 31. Hannover.

Barr, N. (1998). *The economics of the welfare state.* Oxford: Oxford Univ. Press.

Baumol, W.J., Oates, W.E. (1995). *The theory of environmental policy.* Sec. ed., repr., Cambridge: Cambridge Univercity Press.

Becker, U., Gerike, R., Rau, A., Zimmermann, F. (2002). *Ermittlung der Kosten und Nutzen von Verkehr in Sachsen – Hauptstudie.* (Determination of external costs of transport for Saxony – main study). On behalf of Saxon department for Environment and Geology. Final report, Dresden.

Becker, U. (Ed.) (2001). *Gesellschaftliche Ziele von und für Verkehr – Was ist die Aufgabe unserer Verkehrssysteme, und wie sollen sie gestaltet werden?.* Documentation of the workshop (10/10/2000, Taschenbergpalais in Dresden). Dresden.

Becker, U., Gerike, R., Völlings, A. (1999). *Gesellschaftliche Ziele von und für Verkehr* (Societal goals for the transport sector). Issue 1 of the papers of Dresden Institute for Transportation and Environment (DIVU). Dresden.

Berger, W. (1992). *Das Bedürfnis und sein Schatten – Vorarbeiten zu einer philosophischen Anthropologie.* München.

Birnbacher, D. (1999). *Kommentargutachten. Beauftragt im Rahmen des HGF-Projekts „Untersuchung zu einem integrativen Konzept nachhaltiger Entwicklung. Bestandsaufnahme, Problemanalyse, Weiterentwicklung".* Düsseldorf.

Birnbacher, D. (1996). *Ökologie und Ethik*. Reclam: Stuttgart.

Birnbacher, D. (1979). *Was wir wollen, was wir brauchen und was wir wollen dürfen.* In: Meyer-Abich, 1979, pp. 30-57.

Blotevogel, H.H. (Ed.) (2002). *Fortentwicklung des Zentrale-Orte-Konzepts*. Hannover, Academy for Spatial Research and Planning, (Forschungs- und Sitzungsberichte / ARL, Vol. 217).

Blum, U. (2000). *Volkswirtschaftslehre - Studienhandbuch*. München, Wien: Oldenbourg.

Borchard, K. (1974). *Der Flächenbedarf der Siedlung und ihre Folgekosten*. Institue for Urabn design and Housing, Academy for Spatial Research and Planning (Ed.). München.

Borken, J. (2005). *Umweltindikatoren als ein Instrument der Technikfolgenabschätzung –Selektion, Aggregation und multi-kriterielle Bewertung am Beispiel des Verkehrs.* PhD thesis, Universität Freiburg/Breisgau, http://www.freidok.uni-freiburg.de/volltexte/1938/.

Brösse, U. (1999). *Einführung in die Volkswirtschaftslehre, Mikroökonomie*. München, Wien: Oldenbourg.

Brösse, U. (1982). *Raumordnungspolitik*. Berlin: de Gruyter.

Brown-Weiss, E. (1989). *In Fairness to Future Generations. International Law, Common Patrimony and Intergenerational Equity*. New York.

Brundtland, G. (Ed.) (1987). *Our common future: The World Commission on Environment and Development.* Oxford: University Press Oxford.

Buchanan, J.M., Musgrave, R.A. (2001). *Public Finance and Public Choice – Two Contrasting Visions of the State.* Cambridge, London: MIT Press.

BUND/Miserior (Ed.) (1996). *Zukunftsfähiges Deutschland – Ein Beitrag zu einer global nachhaltigen Entwicklung.* Basel, Boston, Berlin: Birkhäuser.

Bundesministerium für Raumordnung, Bauwesen und Städtebau (Ed.) (1995). *Nachbarschaftsladen 2000 als Dienstleistungszentrum für den ländlichen Raum.* Berlin.

Bundesregierung (2002). *Perspektiven für Deutschland – Unsere Strategie für eine nachhaltige Entwicklung.* Berlin. http://www.dialog-nachhaltigkeit.de.

Carlowitz, H. C. von (1713). *Sylvicultura oeconomica oder Haußwirtschaftliche Nachricht und naturgemäße Anwendung zur wilden Baum-Zucht.* Leipzig: Braun, (Reprint: TU Bergakademie Freiberg, Universitätsbibliothek, Nr. 135, Freiberg, 2000).

Chen, G. (Ed.) (2003). *Chaos control – theory and applications.* Berlin, Heidelberg: Springer.

Constanza, R. et al. (2001). *Einführung in die Ökologische Ökonomik*. Stuttgart: Lucius & Lucius.

Daly, H.E. (1996). *Beyond Growth – The Economics of Sustainable Development.* Beacon Press, Boston.

Daly, H.E. (1992). Allocation, Distribution and scale: Towards an Economic that ist Efficient, Just and Sustainable. In: *Ecological Economics*, Vol. 6, pp. 185-193.

Danielzyk, R., Koch, R. (2001). *Pilotstudie zur Steuerungswirksamkeit des Zentrale-Orte-Konzepts.* On behalf of Academy for Spatial Research and Planning (ARL). Hannover.

Decker, J. (2001). *Nachhaltigkeit im Verkehrsbereich durch netzgestützte kooperative Planungs- und Entscheidungsunterstützung.* Clausthal: Papierflieger Verlag.

German Society of Transport Science (Deutsche Verkehrswissenschaftliche Gesellschaft e.V., DVWG) (Ed.) (2001). *Kommunikation und Beteiligung bei Verkehrsprojekten – Beschleunigung oder Behinderung?.* Materials to the scientific congress, 28/9/2000, Wuppertal (scientific series of DVWG, vol. B 233).

Diefenbacher, H. (2001). *Gerechtigkeit und Nachhaltigkeit – Zum Verhältnis von Ethik und Ökonomie.* Darmstadt: Wiss. Buchgesellschaft.

Diekmann, A., Voss, T. (2004). *Rational-Choice-Theorie in den Sozialwissenschaften, Anwendungen und Probleme.* München: Oldenbourg.

Dienel, P.C. (2002). *Die Planungszelle – Der Bürger als Chance.* Opladen: Westdeutscher Verlag.

Dolgoff, R., Feldstein, D. (2006). *Understanding Social Welfare: A Search for Social Justice.* Allyn & Bacon.

Dom, A., Ridder, W. de (2002). *Paving the way for EU enlargement. Indicators of transport and environment integration - TERM 2002.* European Environment Agency. Kopenhagen.

Druwe, U., Kunz, V. (Ed.) (1999). *Politische Gerechtigkeit.* Opladen: Leske + Budrich.

Eichmann, V., Berschin, F., Bracher, T., Winter, M. (2006). *Umweltfreundlicher, attraktiver und leistungsfähiger ÖPNV – ein Handbuch.* Berlin: DifU.

Ekardt, F. (2004). *Zukunft in Freiheit.* Leipzig: Schleussig.

Empacher, C., Wehling, P. (2002). *Soziale Dimensionen der Nachhaltigkeit – Theoretische Grundlagen und Indikatoren.* Papers of ISOE no. 11. Frankfurt a.M.

Endres, A. (1993). *Die Ökonomie natürlicher Ressourcen: Eine Einführung.* Darmstadt: Wiss. Buchges.

Enquête-Kommission des Deutschen Bundestages, Zukunft des Bürgerschaftlichen Engagements (Ed.) (2002). *Bürgerschaftliches Engagement und Zivilgesellschaft.* Opladen: Leske + Budrich.

Enquête-Kommission „Zukunft der Mobilität", Landtag Nordrhein-Westfalen, 12. Wahlperiode (2000). *Die Zukunft der Mobilität in Nordrhein-Westfalen.* Düsseldorf.

Epp, A. (1998). *Divergierende Konzepte von „Verfahrensgerechtigkeit" - Eine Kritik der Procedural Justice Forschung.* In: Discussion Paper FS II 98-302. Social Science Research Center Berlin.

Eppler, E. (2000). *Was braucht der Mensch? – Vision: Politik im Dienst der Grundbedürfnisse.* Frankfurt a.M., New York: Campus.

Erikson, S.H. (1968). *Kindheit und Gesellschaft.* Stuttgart.

Ettema, D., Timmermans, H. (Ed.) (1997). *Activity-based Approaches to Travel Analysis.* Pergamon.

Ewers, H.-J. (1996). Dauerhaft-umweltgerechte Mobilität. In: Barz, W. (Ed.) *Umwelt und Verkehr: Symposium on June 19th and 20th, 1995 in Münster*. Landsberg: ecomed.

Farley, J., Daly, H. E. (2005). *Ecological Economics: A Workbook For Problem-Based Learning*. Island Press.

Farley, J., Daly, H. E. (2003). *Ecological Economics: Principles And Applications*. Island Press.

Federal Ministry of the Interior (2004). *"Modern State—Modern Administration"*. Strategy for Modernizing the Federal Administration. Phase 2 of the Government Programme. Berlin, 2004, http://www.staat-modern.de.

Federal Statistical Office (Ed.) (1996). *Wohlfahrtsmessung – Aufgabe der Statistik im gesellschaftlichen Wandel*. Documentation of the scientific colloquium, 1995, Nov 16 and Nov 17, Wiesbaden. Stuttgart: Metzler-Pöschel.

Feindt, P. H. (Ed.) (2005). *Partizipation, Öffentlichkeitsbeteiligung, Nachhaltigkeit – Perspektiven der politischen Ökonomie*. Marburg: Metropolis.

Feldman, A. M. (1997). *Welfare economics and social choice theory*. Boston [u.a.]: Kluwer-Nijhoff.

Forschungsgesellschaft für Straßen- und Verkehrswesen (FGSV), Arbeitsausschuss Grundsatzfragen der Verkehrsplanung (2002). *Beurteilung und Abwägung in der Verkehrsplanung mit Hilfe des Formalisierten Abwägungs- und Rangordnungsverfahrens (FAR)*. FGSV-working paper no. 58. Köln.

Forschungsgesellschaft Straßen- und Verkehrswesen, Arbeitsgruppe Verkehrsplanung (FGSV) (2000). *Leitfaden für Verkehrsplanungen*. Köln.

Forschungsgesellschaft für Straßen- und Verkehrswesen (FGSV), Arbeitsgruppe Verkehrsplanung (1992). *Hinweise zur Anwendung der Richtlinien für die Anlage von Straßen (Teile RAS-N, L, Q, K) beim Um- und Ausbau von Straßen in den neuen Bundesländern*. Köln.

Forschungsgesellschaft für Straßen- und Verkehrswesen (FGSV), Arbeitsgruppe Verkehrsplanung (1988). *Richtlinien für die Anlage von Straßen RAS, Teil: Leitfaden für die funktionale Gliederung des Straßennetzes RAS-N*. Köln.

Freistaat Sachsen, Sächsisches Staatsministerium des Innern (Ed.) (2003a). *Landesentwicklungsplan 2003*. Dresden.

Freistaat Sachsen, Sächsisches Staatsministerium des Innern (Ed.) (2003b). *Landesentwicklungsbericht 2002*. Dresden.

Freistaat Sachsen, Staatsministerium für Umwelt und Landesentwicklung (Ed.) (1994). *Landesentwicklungsplan Sachsen*. Dresden.

Friedman, J. (Ed.) (1996). *The Rational Choice Controversy – Economic Models of Politics Reconsidered*. New Haven, London Yals: University Press.

Fritsch, M., Wein, T., Ewers, H.-J. (2005) *Marktversagen und Wirtschaftspolitik: Mikroökonomische Grundlagen staatlichen Handelns*. München: Vahlen.

Gasieth, S. (1981). *Menschliche Bedürfnisse. Eine theoretische Synthese*. Frankfurt a.M.

Galtung, J. (1980). The Basic Needs Approach. In: Lederer, K. (Ed.) *Human needs – A contribution to current debate.*

Gerhardt, V. (2007). *Partizipation. Das Prinzip der Politik.* Beck.

Gerike, R. (2005). *Wie kann das Leitbild nachhaltiger Verkehrsentwicklung konkretisiert werden? – Ableitung grundlegender Aufgabenbereiche* (How to bring the concept of sustainable development into real life? – Development of constitutive tasks fields). Ph.D-thesis. TU Dresden, Dresden, http://www.divu.de/, http://hsss.slub-dresden.de/hsss/servlet/hsss.urlmapping.MappingServlet?id=1132862870193-1270.

Von Gottl-Ottlilienfeld, F. (1928). *Bedarf und Deckung – Ein Vorgriff in Theorie der Wirtschaft als Leben.* Jena: Gustav Fischer.

Grunwald, A., Kopfmüller, J. (2006). *Nachhaltigkeit.* Campus.

Gudmundsson, H. (2004). *Sustainable Transport and Performance Indicators.* Issues in Environmental Science and Technology. no. 20. Transport and the Environment, pp. 36-63.

Hammer, A., Scheiner, J. (2002). *Lebensstile, Milieus und räumliche Mobilität.* Technical Note for the project „StadtLeben", work package1 + 2.

Hanusch, H. (1994). *Nutzen-Kosten-Analyse.* München: Vahlen.

Hauser, R. (1996). Zur Messung individueller Wohlfahrt und ihrer Verteilung. In: Federal Statistical Office (Ed.). *Wohlfahrtsmessung – Aufgabe der Statistik im gesellschaftlichen Wandel.* Documentation of the scientific colloquium, 1995, Nov 16 and Nov 17, Wiesbaden. Stuttgart: Metzler-Pöschel.

Haustein, D, Manz, G. (1976). *Bedürfnisse, Bedarf, Planung.* Berlin: Verlag Die Wirtschaft.

Heiland, S., Tischer, M., Döring, T., Pahl, T., Jessel, B. (2003). *Indikatoren zur Zielkonkretisierung und Erfolgskontrolle im Rahmen der Lokalen Agenda 21.* UBA-Texte 67/03. Berlin.

Heinemann-Knoch, M. (1977). *Stadtplanung als Praxis der Bedürfnisbefriedigung.* Augsburg: Maro.

Hermann, F.B.W. von (1870). *Staatswirtschaftliche Untersuchungen.* München.

Hessisches Ministerium für Wirtschaft, Verkehr, Technologie und Europaangelegenheiten (Ed.) (1994). *Der Nachbarschaftsladen: Alles unter einem Dach!.* Wiesbaden.

Holstein, L. (2003). *Nachhaltigkeit und neoklassische Ökonomik.* Marburg: Metropolis.

Holz-Rau, C., Jansen, U. (2006). Mobilitätssicherung durch energiesparsame integrierte Siedlungs- und Verkehrsplanung. In: *Informationen zur Raumentwicklung,* Heft 8.2006, pp. 447-456.

Holz-Rau, C. (2002). Integrierte Verkehrsplanung – Eine lange Geschichte. In: *Planungsrundschau* 05/2002.

Hondrich, K. O., Randolph, V. (1983). *Bedürfnisse im Wandel: Theorie, Zeitdiagnose, Forschungsergebnisse.* Westdeutscher Verlag: Opladen.

Holtkamp, L., Bogumil, J., Kißler, L. (2006). *Kooperative Demokratie. Das politische Potenzial von Bürgerengagement.* Campus.

Institut für Landes- und Stadtentwicklungsforschung des Landes Nordrhein-Westfalen (ILS) (Ed.) (2001). *Neue Formen der Kommunikation und Kooperation im Städtebau – Eine Arbeitshilfe für die Praxis.* in Zusammenarbeit mit der Bauministerkonferenz. ils-Bausteine 23. Dortmund.

Infras/IWW (2004). *External Costs of Transport – Update Study.* On behalf of the International Union of Railways (UIC). Final Report. Zürich.

Israel, J. (1985). *Der Begriff der Entfremdung – Zur Verdinglichung des Menschen in der bürokratischen Gesellschaft.* Reinbek bei Hamburg.

Jeon, C. M., Amekudzi, A. (2005). Addressing Sustainability in Transportation Systems: Definitions, Indicators, and Metrics. In: *Journal of infrastructure systems,* March 2005, pp. 31-50.

Jörissen, J., Kopfmüller, J., Brandl, V., Paetau, M. (1999). *Ein integratives Konzept nachhaltiger Entwicklung.* Karlsruhe.

Johansson, P.-O. (1991). *An introduction into modern welfare economics.* Cambridge: Cambridge University Press.

Junker, R., Kühn, G. (2006). *Nahversorgung in Großstädten.* German Institute of Urban Affairs (DifU). Berlin.

Kastenholz, H.G., Erdmann, K.-H., Wolff, M. (Eds.) (1996). *Nachhaltige Entwicklung – Zukunftschancen für Mensch und Umwelt.* Berlin, Heidelberg u.a.: Springer.

Keller, P. (2002). *Mehr Mobilität mit weniger Verkehr eine Herausforderung der Zukunft – Einige Thesen.* (Arbeitsberichte Verkehrs- und Raumplanung, 143, Zürich, 2002). http://www.ivt.baug.ethz.ch/vrp/arbeitsberichte_d.html.

Kentmann, K. (1980). *Nutzungsuntergrenzen der Infrastruktur in ländlichen Räumen.* Hannover: Schroedel.

Kirchgässner, G. (2000). *Homo Oeconomicus – Das ökonomische Modell individuellen Verhaltens und seine Anwendung in den Wirtschafts- und Sozialwissenschaften.* Tübingen: Mohr Siebeck.

Kirchgässner, G. (1997). Nachhaltigkeit in der Umweltnutzung: Einige Bemerkungen, In: *Zeitschrift für Umweltpolitik und Umweltrecht.* In: Beiträge zur rechts-, wirtschafts- und sozialwissenschaftlichen Umweltforschung 20, H. 1, 1997, pp. 1-34.

Knoll, F. (1977). *Bedürfnis – Erziehungswissenschaftliche Reflexion, Implikation und Konsequenz.* München, PhD-thesis.

Koch, R., Stein, A. (2001). *Kommunale Entwicklungsstrategien in der Region Dresden – Hintergründe und Bedeutung für die Verwirklichung verkehrssparsamer Siedlungsstrukturen.* Ed.: TU Hamburg-Harburg, European Centre for Transportation and Logistics, ECTL Working Papers 5.

Köberlein, C. (1997). *Kompendium der Verkehrspolitik.* München, Wien: Oldenbourg.

Kopfmüller, J. et al. (2001a). *Nachhaltige Entwicklung integrativ betrachtet – Konstitutive Elemente, Regeln, Indikatoren.* Berlin: ed. Sigma.

Kopfmüller, J. et al (2001b). *Forschungswerkstatt Nachhaltigkeit – Wege zur Diagnose und Therapie von Nachhaltigkeitsdefiziten.* Berlin: ed. Sigma.

Krech, D., Crutchfield, R.S. (1968). *Grundlagen der Psychologie*. Vol. 1. Berlin: Weinheim.

Kreuzburg, J. (1999). *Ökonomisches Effizienzkriterium und umweltpolitische Zielbestimmung*. Marburg: Metropolis.

Laaser, C.-F. (1991). *Wettbewerb im Verkehrswesen – Chancen für eine Deregulierung in der Bundesrepublik*. Tübingen.

Land Berlin, Senatsverwaltung für Stadtentwicklung, Abteilung VII Verkehr (2001). *Nahverkehrsplan Berlin 2000/2001 und 2004*. http://www.stadtentwicklung.berlin.de.

Lederer, K. (Ed.) (1980). *Human needs. A contribution to the current debate*. Königstein/Ts.: Cambridge/Mass.

Lerch, A., Nutzinger, H.G. (2000). Sustainability: economic approaches and ethical implications. In: *Volkswirtschaftliche Diskussionsbeiträge* 12/00, Universität Gesamthochschule Kassel, Fachbereich Wirtschaftswissenschaften, Kassel, http://www.uni-kassel.de/fb7/ivwl/diskussionsbeitraege/index.html.

Lenz, K. (2000). *Kindsein in Dresden – Endbericht der Ersten Dresdner Kinderstudie*. Technische Universität Dresden. Forschergruppe Kinder- und Jugendforschung. Dresden.

Liebig, S., Lengfeld, H. (Ed.) (2002). *Interdisziplinäre Gerechtigkeitsforschung – Zur Verknüpfung empirischer und normativer Perspektiven*. Frankfurt, New York: Campus.

Link, H. (2005). Transport accounts—methodological concepts and empirical results. In: *Journal of Transport Geography* 13 (2005), pp. 41-57.

Litman, T.A. (2006a). *Evaluating transportation equity – guidance for incorporating distributional impacts in transportation planning*. Victoria Transport Policy Institute. http://www.vtpi.org/equity.pdf.

Litman, T.A. (2006b). *Transportation market distortions – a survey*. Victoria Transport Policy Institute. http://www.vtpi.org/distort.pdf.

Litman, T. (2006c). *Whats it worth? Economic evaluation for transportation decision-making*. Victoria Transport Policy Institute. http://www.vtpi.org/worth.pdf.

Litman, T. (2005a). *Well measured. Developing indicators for comprehensive and sustainable transport planning*. Victoria Transport Policy Institute. http://www.vtpi.org/wellmeas.pdf.

Litman, T. (2005b). *Measuring transportation – traffic, mobility and accessibility*. Victoria Transport Policy Institute. http://www.vtpi.org/measure.pdf.

Litman, T. (2003). *Social inclusion as a transport planning issue in Canada*. Contribution To The FIA Foundation G7 COMPARISON. Victoria.

Mallmann, C. (1980). Needs and processes, goals and indicators. In: Lederer, K. (Ed.)., *Human needs. A contribution to current debate*.

Marcuse, H. (1979). *Der eindimensionale Mensch. Studien zur fortgeschrittenen Industriegesellschaft*. Darmstadt. Neuwied.

Maslow, A.H. (1987). *Motivation and Personality*. HarperCollins Publishers.

Marx, K., Engels, F. (1976a). Gesamtausgabe (MEGA), Zweite Abteilung, „Das Kapital“ und Vorarbeiten. Bd. 1, Karl Marx: *Ökonomische Manuskripte 1857/58*, Text, Teil 1, Berlin: Dietz.

Marx, K., Engels, F. (1976b). Gesamtausgabe (MEGA), Zweite Abteilung, „Das Kapital“ und Vorarbeiten. Bd. 3, Karl Marx: *Zur Kritik der politischen Ökonomie (Manuskript 1861-1863),* Text, Teil 1, Berlin: Dietz.

Marx, K., Engels, F. (1983). Gesamtausgabe (MEGA), Zweite Abteilung, „Das Kapital“ und Vorarbeiten. Bd. 5, Karl Marx: *Das Kapital – Kritik der politischen Ökonomie Erster Band,* Hamburg 1867, Text, Berlin: Dietz.

Marx, K., Engels, F. (1985). Gesamtausgabe (MEGA), Erste Abteilung, *Werke Artikel Entwürfe 1873 bis 1882.* Bd. 26, Text, Berlin, Dietz Verlag.

Marx, K., Engels, F. (1990). Gesamtausgabe (MEGA), Erste Abteilung, Werke Artikel Entwürfe, Friedrich Engels: *Der Ursprung der Familie des Privateigentums und des Staates.* Bd. 29, Text, Berlin: Dietz.

Mead, G.H. (1991). *Geist, Identität und Gesellschaft aus der Sicht des Sozialbehaviorismus.* Frankfurt a.M.: Suhrkamp.

Menger, C. (1923). *Grundsätze der Volkswirtschaftslehre.* Wien/Leipzig.

Meyer-Abich, K. M., Birnbacher, D. (Eds.) (1979). *Was braucht der Mensch, um glücklich zu sein?: Bedürfnisforschung und Konsumkritik.* München: Beck.

Möller, R. (1978). „Lebenslage“ als Ziel der Politik. In: *WSI-Mitteilungen* Jg. 31, H. 10, 1978, pp. 553-563.

Momberg, R. (2000). *Theorie und Politik der Infrastruktur unter Berücksichtigung institutionen- und politökonomischer Einflussfaktoren.* Frankfurt: Peter Lang.

Moore, J. C. (2006). *General Equilibrium and Welfare Economics.* Springer.

Müller, W., Korda, M. (Eds.) (1999). *Städtebau.* Leipzig, Stuttgart: B.G. Teubner.

Mussel, C. (1992). *Bedürfnisse in der Planung der Städte.* Kassel.

Nagel, G. (1985). *Grundbedürfniskonzepte zur Entwicklungspolitik, Wurzeln- Umriß – Chancen.* München: Minerva.

Nash, C., with contributions from partner (2003). UNITE (UNIfication of accounts and marginal costs for Transport Efficiency). *Final Report for Publication,* Funded by 5th Framework RTD programme, Leeds, http://www.its.leeds.ac.uk/projects/unite/deliverables.html.

Nill, J., Einacker, I., Korbun, T., Nordbeck, R., Peine, A. (2002). *Nachhaltigkeitsstrategien – Sondierung neuerer Ansätze innovativer politischer Langfriststrategien und Ergebnisse einer empirischen Vertiefung im Handlungsfeld Mobilität und Verkehr.* Institute for Ecological Economy Research.

Niskanen, E. (2003). *TIPP – Approach to Analysing Institutional Issues in Transport Policy Implementation.* Del. 1, Final draft, 4 April 2003, http://www.strafica.fi/tipp/reports.html.

Nuscheler, F. (1996). *Lern- und Arbeitsbuch Entwicklungspolitik.* Bonn.

Nutzinger, H. G. (Ed.) (1996). *Naturschutz – Ethik – Ökonomie: theoretische Begründungen und praktische Konsequenzen.* Marburg: Metropolis.

Osborne, M. J. (2004). *An introduction to game theory.* New York [u.a.]: Oxford University Press.

Pampel, F. (1981). *Empfehlungen für einen Bedienungsstandard im öffentlichen Personennahverkehr.* VÖV-Schriften, Reihe Technik, VÖV 1.41.1. Köln.

Parsons, S. (Ed.) (2002). *Game theory and decision theory in agent based systems.* Boston, Mass. [u.a.]: Kluwer.

Partzsch, D. (1966). *Die Siedlungsstruktur und das Netz der zentralen Orte.* Informationsbriefe für Raumordnung. [R] 2.1.2. Kohlhammer.

Pearce, D., Barbier, E., Markandya, A. (1990). *Sustainable development – economics and environment in the third world.* Aldershot: Edward Elgar.

Persson, T., Tabellini, G. (2000). *Political economics – explaining economic policy.* Cambridge: MIT Press.

Pigou, A. (2006). *The economics of welfare.* Cosimo.

Pound, B. (Ed.) (2003). *Managing natural resources for sustainable livelihoods – uniting science and participation.* London: Earthscan.

Prechtl, P. (1983). *Bedürfnisstruktur und Gesellschaft – Die Problematik der Vermittlung von Bedürfnis des Menschen und gesellschaftlicher Versagung bei Gehlen, Fromm und Marcuse.* Studien zur Anthropologie, Vol. 3, Würzburg: Königshausen + Neumann.

Proost, S. et al. (2004). REVENUE Revenue Use from Transport Pricing. Del. 2, *Theoretical Framework,* http://www.revenue-eu.org/deliverables.htm.

Quinet, E., Vickerman, R. (2004). *Principles of Transport Economics.* Aldershot: Edward Elgar.

Radke, V. (1999). *Nachhaltige Entwicklung. Konzept und Indikatoren aus wirtschaftstheoretischer Sicht.* Heidelberg.

Rasmusen, E. (2005). *Games and information – an introduction to game theory.* Blackwell: Malden.

Rawls, J. (2003). *A theory of justice.* Reprint. Oxford: Oxford Univ. Press.

Renn, O., Kastenholz, H.G. (1996). Ein regionales Konzept nachhaltiger Entwicklung. In: *Gaia* 5 (1996), pp. 86-102.

Ricci, A. (2005). IMPRINT-NET Implementing pricing reforms in Transport – Networking. Del. 1. *Pricing for (sustainable) transport policies – a state of the art.*

Rompuy, J.V. u.a. (2003). SUMMA (SUstainable Mobility, policy Measures and Assessment). Del. 9. *Marginal Costs of Abatement for Environmental Problems Caused by Transport.* http://www.summa-eu.org.

Sabbagh, C. (2002). *Eine Taxonomie normativer und empirischer Theorien der Verteilungsgerechtigkeit.* In: (Liebig, 2002), pp. 23-52.

Schade, J., Schlag, B. (Eds.) (2003a). *Acceptability of transport pricing strategies.* Oxford: Elsevier.

Schade, J., Schlag, B. (2003b). Acceptability of urban transport pricing strategies. In: *Transportation Research Part F: Traffic Psychology and Behaviour,* 6 (1), pp. 45-61.

Schade, J., Schlag, B. (2000). *Acceptability of urban transport pricing.* Vatt Research Report 72. Helsinki.

Scherhorn, G. (1959). *Bedürfnis und Bedarf – Sozialökonomische Grundbegriffe im Lichte der neueren Anthropologie.* Beiträge zur Verhaltensforschung Band 1. Berlin: Duncker und Humblot.

Schlag, B. (2003). Ansätze einer psychologisch fundierten Verkehrsplanung. In: Schlag, B., Heger, R. (Eds.) *Verkehrspsychologie. Mobilität – Verkehrssicherheit – Fahrerassistenz,* Lengerich: Pabst Science Publ.

Schlag, B. (2002a). *Lern- und Leistungsmotivation.* Opladen: Leske + Budrich.

Schlag, B., Megel, K. (2002b). *PROGRESSIVE – Mobilitätsbedürfnisse.* Bericht für das Forschungs- und Technologiezentrum der Bahn AG. Dresden/München.

Schlag, B., Schade, J. (2000). Public Acceptability of traffic demand management in Europe. In: *Traffic Engineering + Control,* Vol. 41, No. 8, Sept. 2000, pp. 314-318.

Schley, F. (2001). *Wege zu mehr Nachhaltigkeit im Verkehr.* Dresden: DIVU.

Schlich, R., Axhausen, K.W. (2003). *Wohnumfeld und Freizeitverkehr eine Untersuchung zur Fluchttheorie.* Arbeitsbericht Verkehr- und Raumplanung, 155, Zürich, http://www.ivt.baug.ethz.ch/vrp/arbeitsberichte_d.html.

Schnabel, W., Lohse, D. (1997). *Grundlagen der Straßenverkehrstechnik und der Verkehrsplanung.* Vol. 1, 2. Berlin: Verlag für Bauwesen.

Schönfelder, S., Samaga, U. (2003). *Where do you want to go today? – More observations on daily mobility. Swiss Transport Research Conference,* STRC 03 Conference Paper, Session Mobility, Monte Verita 2003, http://www.strc.ch.

Schwefel, D. (1978). Grundbedürfnisse und Entwicklungspolitik. In: *Entwicklung und Zusammenarbeit,* 19. Jg (1978) 6.

Sen, A. (2000). *Tanner Lectures in Human Values: The Standard of Living (Tanner Lectures in Human Values).* Cambridge: Cambridge University Press.

Siebert, H. (1983). *Ökonomische Theorie natürlicher Ressourcen.* Tübingen: Mohr.

Smith, A. (2003). *The wealth of nations.* Bantam Classics.

Social Exclusion Unit (SEU) (2003). *Making the Connections – Final Report on Transport and Social Exclusion.* London, http://www.socialexclusionunit.gov.uk/.

Sottoli, S. (1981). *Sozialpolitik und entwicklungspolitischer Wandel in Lateinamerika.* Opladen.

Spinner, W. (1976). *Zu einer allgemeinen Theorie der Bedürfnisse.* PhD-thesis. Tübingen.

German Advisory Council on the Environment (SRU) (2005). *Umwelt und Straßenverkehr. Hohe Mobilität – Umweltverträglicher Verkehr.* Sondergutachten. Berlin, http://www.umweltrat.de/02gutach/downlo02/sonderg/SG_Umwelt_und_Strassenverkehr2005_web.pdf.

Streeten, P. et al. (Ed.) (1981). *First Things First. Meeting Basic Human Needs in Developing Countries.* Ox.

Stiglitz, J. E., Schönfelder, B. (1996). *Finanzwissenschaft.* München, Wien: Oldenbourg.

Suntum van, U. (1986). *Verkehrspolitik.* München: Vahlen.

Surburg, U., Kuntz, N., Richard, J. (2002). *Kommunale Agenda 21 – Ziele und Indikatoren einer nachhaltigen Mobilität.* UBA-Berichte 8/02. Berlin.

Tavasszy, L.A., Burgess, A., Renes, G. (2004). IASON (Integrated Appraisal of Spatial economic impacts of transport projects and policies). Final Publishable Report. *Conclusions and recommendations for the assessment of economic impacts of transport projects and policies.* Del. 10. Delft, http://www.inro.tno.nl/iason.

Thuy, P. (1999). *Sozialstaatsprinzip und Marktwirtschaft.* Bern, Stuttgart, Wien: Haupt.

Tiefbauamt der Stadt Zürich (2002). *Umsetzung der Mobilitätsstrategie Stadt Zürich – Strategiekonformitätsprüfung.* Genehmigt durch den Stab Verkehr am 13. Mai 2002, http://www.mobilitaetskultur.ch.

Trinder, E., Hay, A., Dignan, J., Else, P., Skorupski, J. (1991). Concepts of equity, fairness, and justice in British transport legislation, 1960-88. In: *Environment and planning C*, 1991, Vol. 9, pp. 31-50.

Tschentscher, A. (2000). *Prozedurale Theorien der Gerechtigkeit – rationales Entscheiden, Diskursethik und prozedurales Recht.* Baden-Baden: Nomos-Verl.-Ges.

Turowski, G. (Ed.) (2002). *Spatial planning in Germany – structures and concepts.* Hannover, ARL: Schroedel.

Tyler, T.R. (2000). Social Justice: Outcome and Procedure. In: *International Journal of Psychology*, 35(2), 2000, pp. 117-125.

Federal Environment Agency (UBA) (Ed.) (2002). *Nachhaltige Entwicklung in Deutschland: Die Zukunft dauerhaft und umweltgerecht gestalten.* Berlin: Erich Schmidt.

Federal Environment Agency (UBA) (Ed.) (2001). *Dauerhaft umweltgerechter Verkehr.* German Case study for the OECD-project Environmental Sustainable Transport (EST). Berlin.

Federal Environment Agency (UBA) (1997). *Nachhaltiges Deutschland. Wege zu einer dauerhaft-umweltgerechten Entwicklung.* Berlin.

United Nations (1992). *Agenda 21: Earth Summit – The United Nations Programme of Action from Rio.* http://www.un.org/esa/sustdev/documents/agenda21/english/agenda21toc.htm.

Varian, H. R. (2004). *Grundzüge der Mikroökonomik.* München: Oldenbourg.

Verron, H. (2001). Vier Thesen zum Thema nachhaltige Mobilität. In: Becker, U. (Ed.), *Gesellschaftliche Ziele von und für Verkehr – Was ist die Aufgabe unserer Verkehrssysteme, und wie sollen sie gestaltet werden?*. Documentation of the workshop, 10/10/2000, Taschenberg-Palais in Dresden. Dresden.

Voss, T. (Ed.) (2005). *Schlüsselwerke der Rational-Choice-Theorie.* Wiesbaden: Westdt. Verlag.

Voß, A. (2002). *Nachhaltigkeit in der Energieversorgung – Relevante Stromerzeugungstechniken auf dem Prüfstand.* http://elib.uni-stuttgart.de/opus/volltexte/1999/373/pdf/373_1.pdf.

German Advisory Council on Global Change (WBGU) (1999). *Welt im Wandel: Umwelt und Ethik.* Sondergutachten 1999. Marburg: Metropolis.

Wheeler, S. M., Beatly, T. (Ed.) (2004). *The sustainable urban development reader.* London: Routledge.

Wellisch. D. (2000). *Finanzwissenschaft.* Vol. I – III. München: Vahlen.

Widmer, T., Schenkel, W., Hirschi, C. (2000). *Akzeptanz einer nachhaltigen Verkehrspolitik im politischen Prozess – Deutschland, Niederlande und Schweiz im Vergleich.* Report D13 of NFP41 in Switzerland. Bern.

Wieland, B. (2002). *Economic and Ecological Sustainability – The Identity of Opposites?* Diskussionsbeiträge aus dem Institut für Wirtschaft und Verkehr. 2/2002. http://tu-dresden.de/die_tu_dresden/faku taeten/vkw/iwv/diskuss/2002_2_diskusbtr_ivw.pdf.

Wieland, B. (2001). Verkehrspolitik im (für das?) 21. Jahrhundert. In: *Wissenschaftliche Zeitschrift der TU Dresden* 50 (2001) Heft 5+6, pp. 73-77.

Wiggins, D. (1991). *Needs, values, truth – essays in the philosophy of value.* Oxford: Blackwell.

Wirz, S. (1993). *Vom Mangel zum Überfluß – Die bedürfnistheoretische Frage in der Industriegesellschaft.* ICS-Schriften 27. Münster: Aschendorf.

Wittgenstein, L., Wright, G. H. von (Eds.) (1994). *Vermischte Bemerkungen – eine Auswahl aus dem Nachlass.* Frankfurt a.M.: Suhrkamp.

Zegras, C. (2002). *Private sector participation in urban transport infrastructure provision.* Eschborn. GTZ.

Zundel, S. (1995). Berlin: Duncker & Humblot.

E.2 Catalogue of facilities for central places in Saxony

The catalogue of facilities is taken from the regional development plan of the Free State of Saxony (Freistaat Sachsen, 1994). This catalogue should be understood as long-term orientation. No demands can be derived from it; the public authorities fulfil the orientation within the bounds of economic possibility.

The catalogue of facilities for higher level central places includes the lower levels or modifies them.

1. Small centre

- Primary school
- Kindergarten, after-school care
- General practitioner
- Dentist
- Pharmacy
- Ambulant care
- Youth club
- Cultural events facility
- Restaurant and options for accommodation
- Sports hall
- Public library
- Post office
- Store for covering basic requirements (general store)
- Craftsmen for covering basic requirements
- Local branch of savings bank and insurance provider

2. Lower centre

- Secondary school
- Medical specialists
- Facilities for challenged individuals (ambulant and overnight care, residential establishment, nursing home, shared residences)
- Facilities for elderly welfare (welfare centre, mobile social service, club, day care, assisted living, residential home according to local demand)
- Facilities for family education
- Youth centre
- Sports hall and sports field
- Stores for covering higher-level requirements
- Craftsmen for covering qualified requirements
- Exhibition room
- Savings bank and credit institution

3. Middle centre

- University-track education facilities
- Occupational education centres
- Rehabilitation centre (facilities for education and re-education, hands-on work for challenged individuals)
- Schools and social services for physically and mentally challenged individuals
- Facilities for developing talents (music schools etc.)
- Facilities for adult education
- Open facilities for supporting physically and mentally challenged individuals (early education, information centre, meeting places)

- Partial live-in facilities for physically and mentally challenged individuals (hands-on work, shelter)
- Social services (for supporting education, information for pregnant women and families)
- Residential homes for the elderly
- Hospital for regular demand
- Youth welfare service
- Indoor swimming pool
- Sports and leisure hall with options for spectators
- Special sports facilities (for athletics, etc.)
- Theatre
- Museum
- Public library with scientific book inventory and media centre
- Multifunctional shopping facilities for covering higher-level requirements (department store, specialty store)
- Hotels and other facilities for accommodation
- Cinema
- Shopping centre
- Family centre
- Lower level administrative offices and courts of justice
- Branches of savings bank and credit institutes
- Police office

4. Upper centre

- Facilities for higher education
- Research institutes
- Special schools of supra-regional relevance
- Facilities for professional education (vocational school, vocational school for physically and mentally challenged individuals)
- Facilities for professional development
- Facilities for youth education
- Hospital for professional education and re-education
- Hospital for maximum health care
- Facilities for the social care of foreigners
- Theatre
- Concert hall
- Facilities for congresses and trade fairs
- Museums and art collections (headed by paid professionals)
- Comprehensive shopping facilities for specialised higher requirements
- Large sports stadiums with facilities for athletic events (at least 15,000 seats)
- Large indoor swimming pools appropriate for supra-regional events
- Luxury hotels
- Higher level administrative offices and courts of justice
- Main branches of banks, insurances and other financial organisations
- Scientific library